OH
$#!%
WHAT'S FOR DINNER?

MARIA SANSONE

Published by Familius LLC, www.familius.com
PO Box 1249, Reedley, CA 93654

Familius books are available at special discounts for bulk purchases, whether for sales promotions or for family or corporate use. For more information, contact Familius Sales at orders@familius.com.

Library of Congress Control Number: 2022949393

Print ISBN 978-1-64170-738-1
Ebook ISBN 978-1-64170-984-2
KF 978-1-64170-983-5
FE 978-1-64170-982-8

Printed in China

Edited by Peg Sandkam, Shaelyn Topolovec, and Brooke Jorden
Cover design by Brooke Jorden
Book design by Brooke Jorden and Maggie Wickes

Photography by Katie Ring
Food styling by Stacey Stolman
Images on 9, 10, 14, 20, 23, 36, 48, 75, 76, 91, 94, 115, 120, 129, 133, 137, 142, 145 sourced from Shutterstock

10 9 8 7 6 5 4 3 2 1

First Edition

OH $#!%
WHAT'S FOR DINNER?

No-Fuss Weeknight Recipes You'll Swear By

MARIA SANSONE

CONTENTS

Ride-or-Die Sides. 127

INTRODUCTION

If you ever looked at the clock and thought to yourself, "Oh $#!%, what's for dinner?" well, you're my people and this is your book. I got you. We can do this!

I'm gonna let you in on a little secret: food doesn't have to be complicated to be good. There, I said it. Life is complicated; cooking is not. Now, there are countless cookbooks that'll make you feel otherwise. Ones with complex recipes using hard-to-find ingredients you can't pronounce. This is not that book. Those books are your little black cocktail dress and this book is your comfiest pair of worn-in jeans.

This is a cookbook for real life with approachable recipes that will be in your rotation on the regular. I wrote this book for those

long days when you feel like your hair is on fire and you just can't. Let me be that little voice telling you that you can. Pull out this book and let me help you get a no-fuss meal on the table that you can feel good about.

This is a collection of my dinner time go-tos. Most of the meals in this book are on the table in about thirty minutes (or, in some cases, way less). The goal here is to get 'er done quick and dirty. You won't find any appetizers or desserts because mama don't have time for that on a week-night! Just quick and easy entrées and a few of my ride-or-die sides designed to effortlessly mix and match with your main course.

These are some of my favorite meals that I've had throughout my life, whether a family recipe or something I've eaten on one of my travels. I've taken the food I love and broken it down to be made as simply and efficiently as possible.

Writing this book has been a TRIP! I'm not a writer or a professional cook; I'm just a mom of two with a job and a husband and dirty dishes and piles of laundry (you get the picture) who loves to cook and set out to find the most streamlined way to get my favorite foods on the table for my family. I made this cookbook the good ol' fashioned way. I shopped for groceries, cooked each meal for my family (many, many times!), ate (a lot!), took copious notes, and consistently had a sink overflowing with pots and pans. I tested and tested until these recipes were just right and that's what you're holding now.

For years, I've been working on these recipes with my social media family. Back when my youngest was born, so was an idea. I wanted to marry my loves . . . live broadcasting, family, and cooking. So, one day while making dinner with a baby on my hip and one sitting on the counter, I turned the phone around on me, went live on Facebook . . . and the rest is history.

Since then, I've welcomed you into my kitchen and my life. You've seen the good, the bad, and the often hilarious realities of cooking in a time crunch. You tell me you're hungry for a cookbook! So here she is!

Maybe you know me from social media. Maybe you've seen me in your living room hosting a TV show (that's my day job!) or maybe we're meeting for the first time. So, I figured I'd give you a little background on how this book ended up in your hands.

It started a long time ago, back in my grandparents' tiny kitchen. I grew up in that kitchen. And they weren't like today's grandparents. They were old. Old world and old school. Grandma was 100 percent Italian and made three square meals and a pie every single day! (I'll never know how Grandpa stayed so skinny!) I helped, I watched, and, mostly, I ate. To be a good eater in our family was held in the highest regard! I now refer to those days in Grandma's kitchen as Italian preschool.

But, I learned way more than just cooking. She'd listen to the crackly music on her transistor radio and we would hang. Certainly, I picked up something through osmosis in all those afternoons in that tiny kitchen. Maybe that's why I love to cook so much. Maybe it makes me feel warm and cozy like I did way back when life was simple. You'll find a lot of Grandma's recipes here. Favorites like her Italian spin on mac & cheese and goulash and some good ol' Americana classics like her award-winning meatloaf and creamy mashed potatoes.

And it's not just my grandma's cooking that influenced me—my family is ALL over this book! From my husband's favorite sandwich on the planet, The Josh, to my dad's pizza and fried spaghetti, my mom's chili, Aunt Ray's famous blue cheese dressing, and, of course, the crown jewel, Sansone's Sunday Sauce.

In college, I studied in Italy, where I ate my way through the semester. I gained about fifteen pounds and a whole new love for penne con melanzane e mozzarella (penne with eggplant and mozzarella). You'll find that in the book too! I then moved to NYC, which has arguably the best food scene in the world, and I ate it up! Well, the best I could on a super tight budget. I always loved to entertain, and man, we had some of the best times crammed into my itty-bitty apartment! We'll call this the "research and development" phase. There were plenty of burnt meals, burnt body parts, and epic fails! I still have a scar on my wrist from a pesky chicken piccata that jumped out of the pan (that recipe's in here too!) and one memorable Thanksgiving when I forgot to defrost the turkey and my stuffing recipe fell in the toilet. Or that one brunch, when the toilet exploded and my guests were suddenly wading in sewage. Ahhh, the memories.

With a career as a television host (what I consider to be the most fun job on the planet), I've been fortunate enough to travel the world to tell stories. Thanks to the magic of TV, I've found myself cooking with world-renowned chefs, dining in the finest restaurants, and eating some of the most magnificent food in the universe. From piping-hot ramen in Tokyo (the best thing I've ever had) to all the goulash a girl could eat while touring Hungary. In short, I've been there, eaten that, and got the T-shirt!

Now, I'm a busy mom with a lot on my plate and just trying to feed my family without losing my mind. And on most (okay, some) nights, I even pull it off thanks to a lifetime of trial, error, and these tried-and-true recipes.

These are my greatest hits. If these recipes were records, they'd be worn out. But they never get old. Consider these the classics.

I hope this book will empower you in the kitchen, make your day a little easier, and bail you out the next time you think, "Oh $#!%, what's for dinner?"

xo Maria

CHEAT SHEET

I made this cookbook as easy to navigate as possible. But here are a few things to keep in mind as you're cooking away. I've also added little notes on many of the pages. The type of thing I'd be texting you if you asked for the recipe.

What's so special about "freshly grated Parmesan"?

I call for "freshly grated Parmesan" a lot in this book, and here's what I mean: I want you to get a good hunk of Parmigiano Reggiano. It can be pricey, but when stored properly (in a Ziploc bag or wrapped tightly in aluminum foil), it can stay fresh for months in the refrigerator! So, consider it an investment in your foodie future. You'll see that you can buy it pre-grated, but the flavor is so much better if you freshly grate it yourself. And if you're ever thinking of using that "cheese" in the green can, stop what you're doing and phone a friend! You're better than that and someone needs to tell you.

Why San Marzano tomatoes?

Because you're worth it! San Marzano tomatoes come directly from Naples and reign supreme in terms of quality and flavor, and they can be found in your local supermarket. But be sure to check the labels! Many brands try to pass off "San Marzano-style" tomatoes, so don't be fooled. Only buy if there is a D.O.P. stamp, which means it's a product from Italy. Also, you may be tempted to buy them already crushed to save some time, but this step is for good reason: manually releasing those flavors brings a bigger, fresher flavor than buying them already crushed.

Don't forget the little guys!

Salt and pepper, of course!! They are your friends. And don't be shy when using. I've given salt and pepper measurements for each dish, but I can't tell you how to live your life. Your "too salty" may be my "just right." So, that's my suggestion but take it with a grain of salt. Wink, wink. I use Morton Iodized Salt and McCormick Pure Ground Black Pepper for these recipes.

Don't overcook your pasta!

Please, I beg of you . . . don't serve mushy pasta. Check the box and always set a timer for instructions for al dente! And always, add a generous amount of salt to your pasta water.

I love me some cast iron!

Get yourself a cast iron skillet, and don't be intimidated by taking care of it. It's really not a big deal. They are very reasonably priced and an excellent investment. Be good to it and it'll be good to you. They can last a lifetime! Clean with water and dry really well right away. After it's totally dry, add a bit of cooking oil to the pan and use a paper towel to rub it in.

Everything is better with butter!

For these recipes, I use salted butter, and plenty of it.

Deglaze?

On a few occasions, I ask you to deglaze the pan. All this means is adding liquid like wine or chicken broth to your hot pan, which releases the bits of food on the bottom.

WINNER WINNER CHICKEN DINNER

CHICKEN GYRO BOWL

SERVES 4

Inspired by the classic Greek sandwich, this is a deconstructed version that's fresh and light, but totally satisfying, with some of my favorite Mediterranean flavors. You can make four individual bowls or one big platter and serve it up family-style with warm pita bread for dipping. This technique for baking chicken breasts is the world's easiest and most foolproof way. (It will make a few appearances in this book!) Or better yet, if you have leftovers, skip that step and use up your cooked chicken, lamb, or beef.

TOMATO CUCUMBER SALAD:

1 CUP CHERRY TOMATOES, HALVED

1 LARGE CUCUMBER, DICED

1 SMALL RED ONION, THINLY SLICED

1/2 CUP GREEK VINAIGRETTE DRESSING

SALT AND PEPPER TO TASTE

EASY ROASTED CHICKEN:

1 1/2 POUNDS BONELESS, SKINLESS CHICKEN BREAST OR THIGHS

1 TEASPOON GARLIC SALT

1/2 TEASPOON PEPPER

1/2 TEASPOON PAPRIKA

1 CUP GREEK VINAIGRETTE DRESSING

GYRO BOWL:

4 PIECES PITA BREAD

2 TABLESPOONS OLIVE OIL

1 PACKAGE (16 OUNCES) MIXED GREENS

1 CUP CRUMBLED FETA CHEESE

1 CUP PITTED KALAMATA OLIVES, ROUGHLY CHOPPED

1 CAN (14.5 OUNCES) CHICKPEAS, DRAINED AND RINSED

1 CUP TZATZIKI SAUCE

1/4 CUP ROUGHLY CHOPPED FRESH DILL

1. Preheat oven to 350 degrees.

2. In a medium bowl, toss together the tomato cucumber salad ingredients. Set aside.

3. Place chicken in a large baking dish and top with garlic salt, pepper, paprika, and dressing. Bake uncovered for 45 minutes or until cooked through. Let cool and slice into strips.

4. Arrange pita bread on a baking sheet; drizzle with olive oil and warm in the oven for a few minutes.

5. Arrange some tomato and cucumber salad, sliced chicken, mixed greens, feta cheese, Kalamata olives, and chickpeas in each bowl. Garnish with tzatziki sauce and chopped dill; serve with warm pita.

- If you have time, marinate the chicken in Greek vinaigrette and refrigerate for an hour before baking.

LEMONY CHICKEN PICCATA

When life gives you lemons, add butter . . . and a touch of wine! That always helps. I mean, what's not to love about a lightly fried chicken cutlet covered in a lemon butter sauce? This piccata is perfect as is but great served over pasta or rice. And if you're looking to get extra saucy, just add extra butter and lemon juice.

- -

8 OUNCES UNCOOKED PASTA

1/2 CUP ALL-PURPOSE FLOUR

1 1/2 POUNDS THINLY SLICED CHICKEN
   BREAST

1/2 TEASPOON SALT

1/4 TEASPOON PEPPER

1/4 CUP OLIVE OIL

3 TABLESPOONS BUTTER, DIVIDED

2 LEMONS, DIVIDED

1/4 CUP WHITE WINE

2 TABLESPOONS CAPERS, DIVIDED

1/8 CUP CHOPPED FRESH PARSLEY

1   Cook pasta according to package instructions. Drain and set aside.

2   Add flour to a plate. Pat chicken dry with paper towel, season each side with salt and pepper, then coat each side in flour.

3   Heat oil and 1 tablespoon butter in a large skillet over medium-high heat until very hot. Add chicken to the pan. (You may have to do this in batches so they aren't overcrowded.) Cook for 5 minutes or until the outside is crispy and golden brown. Flip and repeat on other side for 3–5 minutes, or until chicken is cooked through. Set aside chicken and keep warm.

4   Turn heat down to low. Add 1 tablespoon butter, the juice from 1 lemon, the white wine, and 1 tablespoon capers; simmer until heated through.

5   Return pasta to its pot; add 1 tablespoon butter and salt and pepper to taste.

6   Add chicken back to the pan and spoon sauce over the top. Add pasta to the sauce and chicken mixture in portions so it's enough to sop up the sauce nicely.

7   Top with the remaining capers and chopped parsley; serve with sliced lemon.

- Save on clean up! For the preparation of this one, I'm all about paper plates. Use for the flour mixture and cooked chicken so you don't have too many dishes.

CRISPY ROAST CHICKEN
IN AU JUS

When I cook this (which I do pretty much weekly), my husband can smell the deliciousness from the driveway when he gets home. This one will make your neighbors hungry!

GARLIC & HERB SEASONING:

1 TEASPOON GARLIC POWDER

1/2 TEASPOON DRIED ROSEMARY

1/2 TEASPOON DRIED THYME

1/2 TEASPOON PAPRIKA

CHICKEN:

6 BONE IN OR BONELSS, SKIN-ON CHICKEN THIGHS

1/2 TEASPOON SALT

1/4 TEASPOON PEPPER

AU JUS:

2 CUPS CHICKEN BROTH

1 LEEK, SLICED (ONLY THE WHITE AND LIGHT GREEN PARTS)

1 LARGE FENNEL BULB, CUT INTO 6 CHUNKS

3 TABLESPOONS BUTTER

1 LEMON, CUT INTO ROUNDS

JUICE OF 1/2 A LEMON

1. Place an empty 12-inch cast-iron skillet or heavy-bottomed oven-safe skillet in the oven. Preheat oven to 375 degrees.

2. Meanwhile, in a small bowl, mix the garlic and herb seasoning ingredients.

3. Pat chicken dry, season each side with salt and pepper, then sprinkle with seasoning mix and rub in.

4. When the oven temp has reached 375 degrees, carefully remove the hot skillet and transfer it onto the stove over medium-high heat. Add chicken to the hot pan. Cook for 3–4 minutes on each side or until golden brown.

5. Add chicken broth, leek, and fennel to the bottom of the skillet. Distribute butter on top of each piece of chicken and then top each with lemon slices and lemon juice.

6. Return the skillet to the oven and continue cooking, uncovered, for 20–25 minutes or until chicken has reached an internal temp of 165 degrees and fennel is tender. Garnish with remaining lemon slices.

- Fennel is so underrated! I love its fresh anise flavor and celery-like texture. All parts of the fennel are edible, but we're focused on the bulb, which is the bottom, white part of the plant. Remove the fronds, set aside and use to garnish.

FRIED CHICKEN 'N WAFFLE TENDERS

SERVES 4

Chicken and waffles are one of the greatest odd couples. By using pancake mix in your batter for the chicken, you get the best of both worlds in every bite. Layer on top of your favorite store-bought or homemade waffles and drizzle with syrup for a sweet and savory weeknight treat.

- 1 TEASPOON PAPRIKA
- 1 TEASPOON GARLIC POWDER
- 1 CUP PANCAKE MIX
- 1 CUP ITALIAN-STYLE PANKO BREAD CRUMBS
- 1 1/2 POUNDS CHICKEN TENDERS OR BONELESS, SKINLESS CHICKEN BREAST, POUNDED AND CUT INTO THIN TENDERS
- 1 TEASPOON SALT

- 1/2 TEASPOON PEPPER
- 2 EGGS, BEATEN
- VEGETABLE OIL, ENOUGH TO COAT BOTTOM OF PAN
- 4 PRE-MADE WAFFLES
- MELTED BUTTER, FOR SERVING
- MAPLE SYRUP, FOR SERVING

1. Mix paprika, garlic powder, and pancake mix in a large Ziplock bag. Set aside.

2. Season chicken with salt and pepper on both sides. In a large bowl, dredge chicken in eggs, making sure both sides are coated, then add chicken to the Ziplock bag, seal the bag, and shake until the chicken is coated.

3. Heat oil in a large skillet over medium-high heat. Lightly fry chicken on each side until crispy and golden brown on the outside and no longer pink inside. (Cooking time depends on thickness of chicken.) Season with additional salt to taste.

4. Cook waffles according to package instructions. Drizzle melted butter and maple syrup on the waffles; plate with chicken tenders.

- I love the Ziplock trick. This allows the chicken to be perfectly coated with way less mess!

CAN'T-BELIEVE-THEY'RE-BAKED HOT GARLIC WINGS

MAKES 20-24 WINGS

You'll have to taste it to believe it, but baked wings can be just as crispy as fried ones! My Aunt Patty introduced me to this technique, and I've never looked back! With all this flavor, it's a great way to spice up your weeknight dinners, or double the recipe for game day get-togethers. Serve with homemade blue cheese dressing and you're in bar food heaven.

WING MARINADE:

1/4 CUP FRANK'S REDHOT SAUCE

3 TABLESPOONS OLIVE OIL

3 TEASPOONS MINCED GARLIC

2 TEASPOONS CHILI POWDER

1 TEASPOON GARLIC POWDER

1 TEASPOON ONION POWDER

1/2 TEASPOON SALT

1/4 TEASPOON PEPPER

CHICKEN:

2 POUNDS CHICKEN WING DRUMETTES

AUNT RAY'S BLUE CHEESE DRESSING TO TASTE (PAGE 90)

1. Combine wing marinade ingredients in a large Ziplock bag.

2. Place chicken wings in the marinade, a few at a time, shaking to coat each piece. Refrigerate for 1 hour.

3. Preheat oven to 400 degrees.

4. Arrange wings on a baking sheet lined with parchment paper and bake for 1 hour, flipping chicken halfway through.

5. Season with additional salt and pepper to taste. Serve with Aunt Ray's Blue Cheese Dressing.

PERSONAL POT PIES
WITH BUTTERMILK BISCUITS

My grandma's pot pies were EPIC! She made her own pie crust and it just seemed way too labor-intensive for a weekday . . . until now. With a few tweaks and refrigerated biscuits, you can add this Americana classic to your weeknight rotation. Save time by using leftover chicken or even a supermarket rotisserie chicken. Any way you slice it, your family will love you when you put this on the table.

2 TABLESPOONS BUTTER

1 SMALL ONION, FINELY CHOPPED

8 OUNCES BABY BELLA OR WHITE MUSHROOM, SLICED

1/2 TEASPOON SALT, DIVIDED

1/4 TEASPOON PEPPER, DIVIDED

2 TABLESPOONS FLOUR

2 CUPS CHICKEN BROTH

1/2 CUP LIGHT CREAM

2 CUPS FROZEN VEGETABLE MIX (PEAS, CARROTS, GREEN BEANS, CORN), THAWED

2 CUPS COOKED CHICKEN BREAST, CUT INTO BITE-SIZE PIECES

1 CAN OF REFRIGERATED BUTTERMILK BISCUITS

1 EGG

1 TABLESPOON WATER

1   Preheat oven to 350 degrees.

2   Melt butter in a medium skillet over medium-high heat. Sauté the onions until translucent. Add the mushrooms and season with half the salt and pepper. Cook until tender.

3   Mix in the flour. Stir in chicken broth and light cream a little at a time.

4   Add vegetables and chicken; simmer for 10 minutes or until sauce thickens. Season with the remaining salt and pepper.

5   Spoon the mixture into four 12-ounce greased ramekins or small oven-safe bowls, leaving enough room for the biscuit. Place one uncooked biscuit on top of each chicken mixture.

6   Whisk together egg and water then brush on top of biscuits. Bake for 20 minutes or until biscuits are cooked through and the tops are golden brown.

7   Serve the remaining biscuits along with your meal.

- See page 3 for an easy roasted chicken breast recipe; just substitute regular Italian dressing or vinaigrette instead of Greek.

THE WHOLE ENCHILADA

When we lived in Southern California, we were totally spoiled by an abundance of top-notch Mexican restaurants. The menus were packed with many drool-worthy dishes, but I could never stray from my old reliable order—chicken enchiladas! Why mess with success? When we moved, I had to learn to make my favorite takeout . . . well, take *in*. I think this is best served with a spicy margarita (or three!) to get the full SoCal vibe.

2 TABLESPOONS OLIVE OIL

1 MEDIUM WHITE ONION, FINELY CHOPPED

1 POUND COOKED BONELESS, SKINLESS CHICKEN BREAST, SHREDDED

1 CAN (15 OUNCES) BLACK BEANS, DRAINED AND RINSED

2 CUPS FRESH SPINACH

1 CAN (16 OUNCES) RED ENCHILADA SAUCE, DIVIDED

1 CUP SOUR CREAM, PLUS MORE FOR SERVING

2 CUPS SHREDDED MEXICAN BLEND CHEESE, DIVIDED

1/2 TEASPOON SALT

1/4 TEASPOON PEPPER

8 FAJITA-SIZE FLOUR TORTILLAS

1 CUP SALSA VERDE

1 CUP CHOPPED FRESH GREEN ONIONS

1/2 CUP CHOPPED FRESH CILANTRO (OPTIONAL)

HOT SAUCE, FOR SERVING

1   Preheat oven to 375 degrees.

2   Heat oil in a large skillet over medium-high heat and cook onions until translucent. Add shredded chicken, black beans, spinach (a bit at a time), half of the enchilada sauce, sour cream, and 1 cup shredded cheese. Cook for 1 minute or until blended and season with salt and pepper.

3   Coat the bottom of an 11x7 rectangular glass baking dish with a thin layer of enchilada sauce.

4   Take a generous scoop of chicken mixture and place it in the center of each tortilla. Wrap each tortilla and place seam-side down in the baking dish.

5   Cover with remaining enchilada sauce, salsa verde, and remaining shredded cheese. Bake for 20 minutes until bubbly.

6   Allow to cool slightly before removing from the dish. Top with cilantro and serve with sour cream and hot sauce!

- Some grocery stores sell pre-shredded roast chicken. If not, shred cooked chicken with an electric mixer. It's so fast and shreds chicken evenly!

CREAMY CHICKEN PASTA
WITH CAPERS &
SUN-DRIED TOMATOES

SERVES 4

I know I'm not supposed to have favorites, but this is one of my favorite recipes in this book. It's a lick-the-bowl situation for me with these creamy Mediterranean flavors and the one-two punch from the capers and sun-dried tomatoes. It's decadent enough for a special occasion but easy enough for *any* day ending in *y*.

- -

12 OUNCES FARFALLE PASTA (A.K.A. BOWTIE PASTA)

1 1/2 POUNDS THINLY CUT BONELESS, SKINLESS CHICKEN BREAST

1/2 TEASPOON SALT

1/4 TEASPOON PEPPER

1 TABLESPOON OIL RESERVED FROM SUN-DRIED TOMATOES,

1 TABLESPOON BUTTER

5 CLOVES OF GARLIC, MINCED

1/3 CUP DRY WHITE WINE

1/2 CUP HEAVY CREAM

1/2 CUP FRESHLY GRATED PARMESAN CHEESE, PLUS MORE FOR SERVING

1 JAR (8 OUNCES) CHOPPED, OIL-PACKED SUN-DRIED TOMATOES, DRAINED (RESERVE OIL)

1 JAR (3 OUNCES) CAPERS, DRAINED

5 OUNCES FRESH SPINACH

1. Cook pasta according to package instructions for al dente. Drain, reserving a cup of pasta water.

2. Season both sides of the chicken with salt and pepper.

3. Heat oil and butter in a large skillet over high heat. Add chicken and cook for 4–5 minutes on each side or until cooked through. Remove chicken from pan and cut into strips or bite-size pieces. Set aside.

4. Reduce heat to low; add garlic and cook for 1 minute. Deglaze the pan with wine and cook for an additional minute, scraping up the brown bits. Stir in cream and cheese. Add sun-dried tomatoes and capers; simmer until sauce thickens.

5. Return chicken to the pan and toss with the sauce. Increase heat to medium and slowly add pasta along with the reserved cup of pasta water. Add spinach and cook until wilted. Top with additional Parmesan cheese.

GONE
FISHIN'

CHILI LIME FISH TACOS

MAKES 10-12 TACOS

There's nothing like a fish taco on the grill, but if you live in cold weather like I do, you're not firin' up the grill in November, so here's how you can get fresh, restaurant-style fish tacos right in your kitchen—all year round! This technique for cooking fish sealed in parchment paper is called "fish en papillote." It's a foolproof way to cook fish that locks in flavor and steams in its own juices to get perfectly cooked and flavorful fish every time.

- -

1 1/2 POUNDS MILD WHITE FISH (LIKE HALIBUT, SNAPPER, TILAPIA, MAHI MAHI)

1/2 TEASPOON SALT

1/4 TEASPOON PEPPER

1/2 TEASPOON CHILI LIME SEASONING

2 LIMES, DIVIDED

2 TABLESPOONS OLIVE OIL

2 TABLESPOONS CHOPPED FRESH CILANTRO, DIVIDED

12 CORN TORTILLAS

1 AVOCADO, DICED

1 CUP PICO DE GALLO OR SALSA

PICKLED SLAW (PAGE 140)

1   Preheat oven to 400 degrees.

2   Place fish in the center of a large piece of parchment paper. Pat fish dry and season with salt, pepper, and chili lime seasoning.

3   Evenly distribute the juice of 1 lime, the olive oil, and 1 tablespoon of chopped cilantro on top of the fish. Slice half of the second lime into rounds; place slices on top of each piece of fish.

4   Lay another piece of parchment paper on top and crimp the edges of both pieces to tightly seal. Place on a sheet pan and bake in the oven for 15–20 minutes or until it reaches an internal temp of 145 degrees, depending on type and thickness of fish.

5   Fill each tortilla with fish, avocado, pico de gallo, and Pickled Slaw. Drizzle with juice from the remaining lime half and top with remaining cilantro.

- Don't be a hero! Pick up fresh pico de gallo or salsa from the market. You can only make so much at once!

MEDITERRANEAN PAN-FRIED FISH WITH "AWESOME SAUCE"

SERVES 4

Simply put, this sauce is awesome. That's all there is to it. Tomatoes, lemon, wine, and olives!? You're speaking my love language. It's the perfect complement to this delicate, crispy, pan-fried white fish, but it also goes great on chicken, pasta, or eggs. I like to serve this fish on top of a bed of rice to soak up every last drop of the "awesome sauce." And because we all have bigger fish to fry than dinner, you'll have this on the table in twenty minutes!

AWESOME SAUCE:

1/4 CUP OLIVE OIL

1/2 ONION, CHOPPED

2 CLOVES OF GARLIC, MINCED

1/4 CUP WHITE WINE

1 CAN (14.5 OUNCES) DICED OR STEWED TOMATOES, DRAINED

1/4 CUP KALAMATA OLIVES, ROUGHLY CHOPPED

1 TABLESPOON FRESH CHOPPED PARSLEY

1/2 TEASPOON SALT

1/4 TEASPOON PEPPER

FISH:

1 1/2 POUNDS MILD WHITE FISH (LIKE HALIBUT, FLOUNDER, SNAPPER, TILAPIA, MAHI-MAHI)

1/2 TEASPOON SALT

1/4 TEASPOON PEPPER

1/4 CUP OLIVE OIL (OR ENOUGH TO COVER YOUR PAN)

1 TABLESPOON BUTTER

1 LEMON, HALVED

1 TABLESPOON FRESH CHOPPED PARSLEY

1   To make the sauce, heat olive oil in a large skillet over medium-high heat. Add onions and cook for 2–3 minutes or until translucent. Stir in garlic and cook for another minute.

2   Deglaze the pan with wine and let reduce for 2 minutes. Add tomatoes, olives, and parsley. Season with salt and pepper. Reduce heat to a simmer and allow sauce to thicken while preparing fish.

3   Pat fish dry and season with salt and pepper on each side. Heat oil and butter in a large skillet over high heat. Add fish and cook for 5–7 minutes on each side until or until cooked through. (You may have to do this in batches so the fish isn't overcrowded.) Squeeze the juice from half of the lemon on top. Cut the remaining lemon half into wedges for serving.

4   Place cooked fish in a serving dish and finish with Awesome Sauce.

- You could use all the same ingredients and prepare the fish in parchment paper like the Chili Lime Fish Tacos (page 21).

NEW ENGLAND CLAM CHOWDAH

Chowdah is a rite of passage here in New England, and having a "wicked good" one in your bag of tricks will make you a legend. Living in a small seaside town north of Boston, I've had my share of chowder (in the name of research, of course!) and drew on all that wonderful inspiration when I concocted this one. The creamed corn gives it a wonderfully sweet twist, while the bacon adds smokiness without messing with the classic flavors. It seems like it would take all day to make this hearty chowder, but you'll have it on the table in about forty-five minutes!

6 SLICES (8 OUNCES) THICK-CUT BACON, DICED

2 TABLESPOONS BUTTER

2 CELERY STALKS, FINELY CHOPPED

1 MEDIUM YELLOW ONION, FINELY CHOPPED

2 CLOVES OF GARLIC, FINELY CHOPPED

1/2 CUP DRY WHITE WINE

2 TABLESPOONS FLOUR

4 CANS (6 OUNCES EACH) WHOLE OR DICED CLAMS IN THEIR JUICES

1/2 POUND YUKON GOLD POTATOES, DICED INTO BITE-SIZE PIECES WITH SKIN ON

1 TABLESPOON SALT

1/2 TABLESPOON PEPPER, PLUS MORE TO TASTE

1 CAN (14.5 OUNCES) CREAM-STYLE CORN

2 CUPS LIGHT CREAM

2 TABLESPOONS CHOPPED CHIVES, FOR GARNISH

1. Cook bacon in a Dutch oven or large soup pot over medium-high heat for 5 minutes or until crispy. Remove a 1/4 cup of bacon from the pan and set aside on a paper towel for garnish.

2. Add butter to bacon grease. Sauté celery and onion for 5 minutes or until vegetables are tender. Stir in garlic and cook for another minute.

3. Deglaze the pan with wine and scrape brown bits off the bottom of the pan. Sprinkle with flour while stirring constantly for 2 minutes or until thickened.

4. Drain the clams over the pot then set aside. Add the potatoes, salt, and pepper to the pot. Simmer for 15 minutes or until potatoes are very tender, stirring occasionally.

5. Add the reserved clams, creamed corn, and cream. Cook for 10 minutes. Season with additional salt and pepper to taste. Garnish with chives and reserved bacon bits.

6. Serve it like they do here in New England with good ol' oyster crackers.

- If you're feeling adventurous, try using fresh clams! You'll need about 1 1/2 pounds, as well as 1 1/2 cups of clam juice.

PISTACHIO-CRUSTED SALMON

This melt-in-your-mouth salmon is simple enough for a weeknight but sophisticated enough for a dinner party. You can use this super-simple cooking technique but modify the toppings to create countless other flavor combinations. My kids go crazy for a very basic salmon with just butter and lemon. It's healthy, fast, and crazy easy. This one's always in my weeknight rotation.

4 SALMON FILETS (ABOUT 1 1/2 POUNDS), SKIN ON

3/4 TEASPOON SALT

1/4 TEASPOON PEPPER

3 TABLESPOONS DIJON MUSTARD

2 TABLESPOONS HONEY

1 LEMON

2 TABLESPOONS CHOPPED FRESH DILL, DIVIDED

3 TABLESPOONS SOFTENED BUTTER

1 CUP SHELLED PISTACHIOS, CHOPPED

1. Preheat oven to 400 degrees.

2. Pat salmon dry with a paper towel and then season with salt and pepper.

3. In a small bowl, mix mustard, honey, juice from half of the lemon, and 1 tablespoon dill. Fold in softened butter and mix well.

4. Line a baking sheet with parchment paper. Place salmon skin-side down on the parchment paper. Spread the butter mixture over the salmon. Press pistachios into the butter mixture. Bake for 15–20 minutes or until salmon is cooked through.

5. Season with additional salt and pepper to taste. Top with remaining dill, a squeeze of lemon juice, and garnish with remaining lemon, sliced.

- This is excellent on the grill too!

- Chop pistachios by placing them in a Ziplock back and crushing them with a mallet. Go ahead, get out your frustration!

SIMPLE SHRIMP SCAMPI
WITH LEMON LINGUINE

SERVES 4

This dinner is a 10/10 and takes about ten minutes! Shrimp Scampi is quite possibly the quickest entrée you can make. Be sure to get fresh, raw shrimp. I ask for it to be peeled and deveined to save on time and (let's be real) shrimp guts totally gross me out, so that's a no-fly zone for me.

1/2 POUND LINGUINE

3 TABLESPOONS OLIVE OIL, PLUS MORE FOR DRIZZLING

3 TABLESPOONS BUTTER

4 CLOVES OF GARLIC, MINCED

1/2 CUP WHITE WINE

1 1/2 POUNDS LARGE OR JUMBO RAW SHRIMP, PEELED AND DEVEINED

1 LEMON, CUT INTO WEDGES

1/2 CUP CHOPPED FRESH PARSLEY, PLUS MORE FOR SERVING

3/4 TEASPOON SALT

1/4 TEASPOON PEPPER

FRESHLY GRATED PARMESAN CHEESE TO TASTE

1 Cook pasta in salted water according to package instructions for al dente.

2 Heat oil and butter in a large skillet over medium-high heat. Add garlic and sauté for 1 minute, being careful not to burn. Pour wine into the skillet and reduce for 2 minutes.

3 Fold in shrimp and cook until pink. Finish with juice from half of the lemon wedges, parsley, salt, and pepper.

4 Add the pasta to your skillet and toss with the shrimp. Top with a healthy drizzle of olive oil, freshly grated Parmesan cheese, and a sprinkling of parsley. Garnish with remaining lemon, cut into wedges.

- Go the extra mile and get fresh linguine. It's a few extra bucks but totally elevates the dish, tastes homemade, and cooks very fast! You'll find it in the refrigerated section of your market.

LET'S
GET
SAUCY

SPRINGTIME VEGGIE PASTA

SERVES 4 - 6

Springtime in a bowl! This melt-in-your-mouth, fresh, and delicious dish is loaded with seasonal vegetables tossed in pasta with lemony butter sauce and topped with creamy goat cheese. Use these veggies or whatever you have on hand, because you can't go wrong with this quick and light take on the classic Pasta a la Primavera.

- 1 ZUCCHINI, SLICED
- 1 YELLOW SQUASH, SLICED
- 2 CUPS CHERRY TOMATOES
- 1 BUNCH ASPARAGUS, CHOPPED
- 1 BUNCH BROCCOLINI, CHOPPED
- 1 LARGE BELL PEPPER, CUT INTO 1-INCH STRIPS
- 1 LARGE RED ONION, CUT INTO 1-INCH STRIPS
- 1/3 CUP OLIVE OIL, PLUS 2 TABLESPOONS, DIVIDED

- 1/3 CUP BALSAMIC VINEGAR
- 1/2 TEASPOON SALT
- 1/2 TEASPOON PEPPER
- 2 TABLESPOONS BUTTER
- 3 LARGE CLOVES OF GARLIC, MINCED
- 1 LEMON
- 12 OUNCES PASTA OF YOUR CHOICE
- 1 CUP CRUMBLED GOAT CHEESE

1. Preheat oven to 425 degrees.

2. In a large mixing bowl or large Ziploc bag, toss all the vegetables in 1/3 cup olive oil, vinegar, salt, and pepper. Arrange vegetables in a single layer on a sheet pan and roast for 30 minutes or until vegetables are tender and tomatoes are bursting.

3. Meanwhile, heat butter and 2 tablespoons olive oil in a large skillet. Add garlic and sauté for 1 minute. Add juice from half of the lemon, then reduce heat down to low.

4. Cook pasta according to package instructions for al dente; reserve pasta water. When done, use a slotted spoon to mix the pasta, along with some pasta water, into the skillet. Fold in roasted vegetables and their juices and toss with pasta. Sprinkle with goat cheese and gently mix. Season with additional salt and pepper to taste.

5. Top with a bit of lemon zest and garnish with remaining lemon, sliced.

SAUSAGE & BROCCOLINI RIGATONI

In just a few minutes, spicy sausage, fresh broccolini, and cheesy rigatoni come together for a well-balanced meal that is packed full of flavor. For a lighter take, this also tastes great with Italian-style ground chicken instead of pork.

12 OUNCES RIGATONI PASTA

1 POUND GROUND ITALIAN SAUSAGE

3 TABLESPOONS OLIVE OIL

3 CLOVES OF GARLIC, CUT INTO SLIVERS

1 BUNCH BROCCOLINI, ROUGHLY CHOPPED

1/4 TEASPOON SALT

1/2 TEASPOON PEPPER

1 CUP CHICKEN BROTH

1/2 CUP FRESHLY GRATED PECORINO ROMANO CHEESE, PLUS MORE FOR SERVING

CRUSHED RED PEPPER FLAKES (OPTIONAL)

1   Bring a large pot of salted water to a boil. Cook pasta according to package directions for al dente; reserve pasta water.

2   Meanwhile, brown sausage in a large sauté pan over medium-high heat. Remove and set aside. Add olive oil and garlic to the pan and cook for about 1 minute, being careful not to burn.

3   Fold in broccolini and season with salt and pepper. Pour in chicken broth, cover, and cook until broccolini is tender. Return sausage to the pan.

4   Using a slotted spoon, transfer pasta to the sauté pan and toss to coat. Add 1/2 cup pasta water. Cook for an additional minute. Top with freshly grated cheese and stir until creamy. (You can add more pasta water to get it to the consistency you like.)

5   Serve with lots of grated cheese and garnish with crushed red pepper, if desired.

- If you can't find ground Italian sausage, you can use Italian sausage links and remove the casings.

10-MINUTE SPAGHETTI CARBONARA

SERVES 4

This classic recipe for authentic Italian comfort food is tried and true. No butter, no cream, no garlic . . . just a few simple, quality ingredients that you probably have on hand. My dad swears you have to go the traditional Italian way and use guanciale, but I'm here to tell you that regular bacon works just fine. And a busy weeknight is no time to be on a wild goose chase looking for pork cheek! So, bacon it is. By the time the pasta is boiled, this whole dish is as good as done. It's super easy, but timing and method are very important, so I *need* you to focus for *10 minutes*. Capeesh?

1 POUND THICK SPAGHETTI OR BUCATINI

3 EGGS

3/4 CUP FRESHLY GRATED PECORINO
ROMANO CHEESE, PLUS MORE FOR SERVING

1/4 TEASPOON SALT

1 TEASPOON BLACK PEPPER

8 OUNCES THICK-CUT BACON, DICED

1   Bring a large pot of salted water to a boil. Cook pasta according to package directions for al dente; reserve pasta water.

2   Meanwhile, in a mixing bowl, lightly beat the eggs with grated cheese, salt, and pepper. Set aside.

3   Fry bacon in a large frying pan over high heat for 5 minutes or until crispy. Remove from heat.

4   When done, remove pasta from boiling water with a slotted spoon and add to the pan with the bacon. Mix well to coat and immediately add the egg and cheese mixture; toss the pasta completely with the sauce. (You can add more pasta water to get the consistency you like.)

5   Top with additional grated cheese and serve immediately.

- The raw egg will cook from the heat of the pasta, but you don't want the pasta too hot or it'll scramble the egg. So, follow the procedure and you're good!

SANSONE'S SUNDAY SAUCE

MAKES ENOUGH FOR 1 POUND PASTA PLUS 1 PINT

I must admit, I haven't exactly signed off with the entire familia, so sharing this recipe is an "ask forgiveness, not permission" situation. But, here goes . . .

Simply having this sauce simmering on the stove reminds me of Sundays and growing up a Sansone. Like many Italian-American families, Sundays revolved around church and sauce. Sometimes at my parents' house, sometimes at my grandparents' . . . it didn't really matter where we got together; the common denominator was the sauce. Making this keeps my heritage and all those wonderful memories alive. When the sauce "is on" and filling the house with those unmistakable aromas, I can still picture my grandfather in his white undershirt eating a giant plate of spaghetti at the head of the table. After dinner he'd say, without fail, "I'm never eating again, not never ever."

It takes longer than any other recipe in this book, but sauce isn't just supper for us—it's a ceremony! So go ahead and make ahead on Sunday and you've got yourself a key ingredient for a bunch of easy weeknight meals.

. . . .

2 TABLESPOONS OLIVE OIL

1 POUND BONELESS COUNTRY-STYLE PORK RIBS

1 POUND SWEET ITALIAN SAUSAGE LINKS

1/2 POUND GROUND BEEF (80/20)

2 CLOVES OF GARLIC, MINCED

2 CANS (28 OUNCES EACH) GROUND OR CRUSHED TOMATOES

1 CAN (28 OUNCES) TOMATO PUREE

1 TEASPOON GARLIC SALT

1/2 TEASPOON BLACK PEPPER

1 TEASPOON DRIED OREGANO

1 TABLESPOON SUGAR

1   Heat olive oil in a large sauce pot over medium-high heat. Add pork and sausage and cook 3–4 minutes on each side or until the outside is golden brown. Remove and set aside.

2   In the same sauce pot, brown the ground beef. Remove some grease from the pan.

3   Push meat to one side of the pan; add garlic and cook for 1 minute, being careful not to burn. Stir in tomatoes and tomato puree. Return pork and sausage to the pot and add garlic salt, pepper, oregano, and sugar; stir well.

4   Allow sauce to come to a boil, then turn heat down to lowest setting and simmer, uncovered, for *at least* 3 hours. (My family cooks it ALL day, but I've found 3 hours to be the magic number.)

- Make a larger batch by adding another can of tomato puree, and doubling the ground beef.

DAD'S FRIED SPAGHETTI

SERVES 4

This is my dad's all-time favorite food and Sansone family secret for a leftover masterpiece. You can use it with your own leftover spaghetti or even leftovers from a restaurant. The key is taking your time until the spaghetti gets a crispy coating. Normally you *don't* want to burn your food, but, in this case, let 'er rip because the slightly burnt bits are delicious! It amazes me how your leftover pasta takes on a completely different flavor with just a few ingredients and a little patience.

1/4 CUP OLIVE OIL

12 OUNCES LEFTOVER SPAGHETTI (THAT'S BEEN *LIGHTLY* TOSSED IN SANSONE'S SUNDAY SAUCE (PAGE 38) AND REFRIGERATED OVERNIGHT)

1 TEASPOON GARLIC POWDER

1/2 TEASPOON CRUSHED RED PEPPER FLAKES (OPTIONAL)

1/2 CUP FRESHLY GRATED PARMESAN CHEESE

1   Heat oil in a large nonstick skillet over high heat. Add leftover spaghetti to pan. Season with garlic powder and red pepper; reduce heat to medium. Cook for 10 minutes undisturbed or until the edges are slightly crunchy. Toss well and continue to cook another 5 minutes.

2   Scrape the brown bits off the bottom and toss to mix. Top with Parmesan cheese and serve!

- Your pasta must be tossed in sauce and refrigerated overnight or longer. True leftovers! Don't try to make it with freshly cooked spaghetti—it's just not the same

PENNE WITH EGGPLANT & FRESH MOZZARELLA

I just love eggplant, and when I was living in Italy, I ate this almost every day. I didn't speak the language very well, but you better believe I knew how to say, "penne con melanzane e mozzarella" (penne with eggplant and mozzarella). Master that and "vino por favor" and you'll have yourself a fine time in Italy! It's hearty yet fresh, and a simple marinara allows the eggplant to shine.

12 OUNCES PENNE PASTA

1/4 CUP OLIVE OIL

2 CLOVES OF GARLIC, MINCED

1 LARGE EGGPLANT, CUT INTO 1/2-INCH CUBES

1 TEASPOON SALT

1/4 TEASPOON BLACK PEPPER

3 CUPS MARINARA SAUCE (SEE RECIPE FOR MARIA'S MONDAY MARINARA ON PAGE 45), DIVIDED

1 CUP FRESHLY GRATED PARMESAN CHEESE, DIVIDED

1 CUP CUBED FRESH MOZZARELLA CHEESE, CUT INTO 1/2-CUBES

1 TABLESPOON CHOPPED FRESH BASIL

1. Cook pasta according to package directions for al dente. Drain and set aside.

2. Meanwhile, heat oil in a large nonstick sauté pan over medium-high heat. Add garlic and cook for about a minute.

3. Stir in cubed eggplant and season generously with salt and pepper. Add 1/2 cup marinara sauce; cover and cook for 15 minutes or until very tender.

4. Fold in 1/2 cup Parmesan cheese and toss until melted and sticking to the pan. Use a wooden spoon or rubber spatula to scrape up the brown bits.

5. Combine pasta and remaining sauce with eggplant mixture. Add fresh mozzarella and toss. Sprinkle on remaining Parmesan cheese and fresh basil.

- Summer and early fall is the best time to buy eggplant. Look for eggplants with shiny, firm skin. If it's too soft, that means it's overripe and could be bitter.

MARIA'S MONDAY MARINARA

Move over Sunday Sauce! Weeknights are for a simple marinara. This makes enough to have some left over, and around here, we call that, "money in the bank." You'll be so happy to open the fridge on a busy night and see a jar of homemade sauce ready to rock! Plus, it comes in handy for so many other recipes in this book. San Marzano tomatoes are a bit more expensive but a must because they're truly the star of this show. Simmer for at least an hour, but if you have the time, it gets better with every minute.

1/4 CUP OLIVE OIL

1/2 YELLOW ONION, MINCED

3 CLOVES OF GARLIC, MINCED

2 CANS (28 OUNCES EACH) SAN MARZANO WHOLE, PEELED TOMATOES

1 TEASPOON SUGAR

1 TEASPOON SALT, PLUS MORE TO TASTE

1/2 TEASPOON PEPPER

1 TABLESPOON FINELY CHOPPED FRESH BASIL, DIVIDED

FRESHLY GRATED PARMESAN CHEESE, FOR SERVING

1. Heat olive oil in a large sauce pot over medium-high heat. Add onion and cook until translucent. Add garlic and cook for 1 more minute.

2. Stir in tomatoes and their juices. Mash tomatoes with a wooden spoon or potato masher.

3. Increase the heat to high and add sugar, salt, and pepper.

4. Once the sauce reaches a boil, reduce heat to low and simmer uncovered, stirring frequently for *at least* one hour . . . longer if you can swing it.

5. Stir in half of the fresh basil. Season with additional salt and pepper to taste.

6. Serve with freshly grated Parmesan cheese and garnish with remaining basil.

STIR THE SAUCE!

- A common phrase shouted across rooms in many Italian households (if ya know, ya know!). If you don't give it a frequent good stir, it'll burn and you'll end up with black bits floating about in your beautiful sauce. So, let this be a cautionary tale and "stir the sauce!"

LAZY LASAGNA

Lasagna involves a lot of TLC and that's part of what makes it so special. I'm happy to take the time and energy to prepare a good old fashioned lasagna on a holiday or even on a Sunday, but mama has no time for that on a weeknight! So, I found a way to streamline the process and still get all the same great flavor by using frozen cheese raviolis instead of cooked lasagna noodles. No need to precook them at all! Just line the raviolis up in your dish and let the oven do the work for you!.

1 POUND GROUND BEEF (80/20)

1 TEASPOON SALT

1/4 TEASPOON PEPPER

4 CUPS OF YOUR FAVORITE SPAGHETTI SAUCE (I RECOMMEND SANSONE'S SUNDAY SAUCE ON PAGE 38), DIVIDED

1 CUP FRESHLY GRATED PARMESAN CHEESE, PLUS MORE FOR SERVING

2/3 CUP ITALIAN-STYLE BREAD CRUMBS

1 CUP CHOPPED FRESH SPINACH

24 (30 OUNCE PACKAGE) LARGE FROZEN CHEESE RAVIOLIS

3 EGGS

12 THICK SLICES MOZZARELLA CHEESE

1   Preheat oven to 350 degrees.

2   In a large skillet over medium-high heat, brown the beef. Season with salt and pepper, then mix in 1 cup of sauce. Remove from heat.

3   In a large mixing bowl, combine Parmesan cheese, bread crumbs, spinach, and egg. Fold in ground beef and sauce mixture. Mix well.

4   In a 9x13 oven-safe baking dish, spread 1 cup of sauce to cover the bottom. (This is very important so the raviolis don't stick!) Layer half of the frozen raviolis, half of the meat mixture, another cup of sauce, and half of the mozzarella cheese. Repeat another layer with the remaining ingredients.

5   Cover the baking dish with aluminum foil and bake for 30–40 minutes or until the inside is bubbly. In the last few minutes, remove aluminum foil and broil to get the cheese golden brown (but not burnt!).

6   Serve with Parmesan cheese.

- One time I asked my Uncle Tim if he ever made his lasagna vegetarian. He said, "If you ever get the urge to do that, you pick up the phone and you call someone." Needless to say, we don't do veggie lasagna in the Sansone family.

ROASTED CAPRESE PASTA

This is everything I love about Caprese Salad but with a roasted twist. It's best with tomatoes noted for their sweetness, like cherry or grape tomatoes. It's super versatile and, while it's delicious tossed with pasta, you could just eat it by the spoonful or serve alongside crusty bread, bruschetta style.

12 OUNCES PASTA OF YOUR CHOICE

2 PINTS CHERRY OR GRAPE TOMATOES

2 CLOVES OF GARLIC, MINCED

1/4 CUP OLIVE OIL

2 TABLESPOONS BALSAMIC VINEGAR (MORE FOR SERVING)

1/2 TEASPOON SALT

1/4 TEASPOON PEPPER

1/4 CUP CHOPPED FRESH BASIL, DIVIDED

8 OUNCES FRESH MOZZARELLA, CUBED

1/2 CUP FRESHLY GRATED PARMESAN CHEESE

1. Preheat oven to 400 degrees.

2. Bring a salted pot of water to a boil and cook pasta according to package instructions. Drain and set aside.

3. Combine tomatoes, garlic, olive oil, vinegar, salt, pepper, and half of the basil on a large sheet pan. Toss to coat. Roast for 15 minutes until tomatoes are bursting.

4. Transfer into a large serving bowl. Season with additional vinegar, to taste, and toss with pasta. Add mozzarella and Parmesan cheese. Top with remaining basil.

- Can be served hot or cold. If I'm serving it cold, I like to add chopped veggies, salami, and cheese and serve it like a pasta salad.

WHERE'S
THE
BEEF

COUSIN GINGER'S MEATBALLS

This is the only meatball recipe you'll ever need. They are famous in my family, and it took some major reconnaissance work to squeeze this recipe out of my cousin. Cousin Ginger is as legendary as her meatballs. She's bold, she's spicy, and she's never been accused of being boring! Same for her meatballs. Drop into your favorite red sauce and serve with pasta, or put them between a bun topped with provolone cheese to make an irresistible meatball slider.

1 MEDIUM YELLOW ONION, QUARTERED

3 CLOVES OF GARLIC

1 CUP ITALIAN PARSLEY, STEMS REMOVED

1 1/2 POUNDS GROUND BEEF (80/20)

1 CUP ITALIAN-STYLE BREAD CRUMBS

1/2 CUP FRESHLY GRATED PARMESAN CHEESE

1 EGG

2 TABLESPOONS RED WINE

1 TEASPOON GARLIC POWDER

1 TEASPOON SALT

1/2 TEASPOON PEPPER

1 Preheat oven to 350 degrees. Spray a large sheet pan with nonstick cooking spray.

2 In a food processor fitted with a steel blade, add onion, garlic, and parsley; process until smooth. Transfer to a large mixing bowl, add ground beef, bread crumbs, cheese, egg, wine, garlic powder, salt, and pepper.

3 Gently mix ingredients with your hands, being careful not to overwork the meat. Roll into 1 1/2-inch balls and place on the sheet pan. Bake for 30 minutes or until firm.

4 Drop into your favorite sauce and garnish with chopped parsley.

- If you don't have a food processor, finely mince the onion, garlic, and parsley. You don't want chunks in your meatballs!

CITY "CHICKEN"

Spoiler alert . . . what you're about to make is *not* chicken. Plot twist—it's pork! Crispy on the outside and tender on the inside, it's easy to see why City Chicken has been a family favorite for so long. In my hometown of Erie, Pennsylvania, this Polish-American dish is common comfort food! My grandfather was Polish and my grandma made this all the time. This mouthwatering recipe has roots in Pittsburgh (not far from where I grew up) and dates back to the Great Depression when pork and veal scraps were more affordable than chicken. Serve with a simple green salad or tomato cucumber salad (page 3) and a side of applesauce to get the total down-home Pennsylvania experience.

2 POUNDS BONELESS COUNTRY-STYLE
  SPARERIBS, CUT INTO 1 1/2-INCH CUBES

1/2 TEASPOON LAWRY'S SEASONED SALT

1/2 TEASPOON PEPPER

2 EGGS

2 TABLESPOONS MILK

4 WOODEN SKEWERS

1 CUP ITALIAN-STYLE BREAD CRUMBS

2 TABLESPOONS OLIVE OIL

1 CUP WATER

1 CHICKEN BOUILLON CUBE

2 TABLESPOONS CHOPPED FRESH PARSLEY

1. Preheat oven to 350 degrees.

2. Place pork on a clean cutting board and pat dry. Sprinkle with seasoned salt and pepper.

3. In a large bowl, whisk eggs and milk together. Add cubed pork and coat.

4. String the cubes onto skewers.

5. Pour bread crumbs onto a plate and dredge the pork skewers until completely coated.

6. Heat olive oil in a large skillet over high heat. When oil is screamin' hot, add pork skewers and cook 2 minutes on each side until brown and crispy.

7. Place water and an uncooked bouillon cube on the bottom of a large oven-safe baking dish. Top with pork skewers. Cover with aluminum foil and place in the oven. Bake for 20–25 minutes or until pork is cooked through but still nice and tender.

8. Spoon the juices over the pork, and top with parsley and additional salt and pepper, to taste.

- In Pennsylvania, this dish is so common, you can find pork already cubed. But for the rest of us, ask the butcher if they'll cube boneless country-style spareribs or boneless pork chops for you.

COZY COTTAGE PIE

Sometimes you just need total comfort food—and this is it! It's like shepherd's pie but with ground beef instead of lamb. Make your mashed potatoes ahead of time or use pre-made (I won't tell!) and this dinner is easy as pie!

1 TABLESPOON OLIVE OIL

1 1/2 POUNDS GROUND BEEF (80/20)

1 MEDIUM ONION, FINELY CHOPPED

2 CUPS FROZEN VEGETABLE MIX (PEAS, CARROTS, GREEN BEANS AND CORN)

1 TEASPOON ONION POWDER

1 TEASPOON GARLIC POWDER

1 TEASPOON SALT

1/2 TEASPOON PEPPER

1 CUP DRY WHITE WINE

1 TABLESPOON TOMATO PASTE

2 TABLESPOONS WORCESTERSHIRE SAUCE

1 CUP CHICKEN BROTH

1 CUP SHREDDED CHEDDAR CHEESE

4 CUPS COOKED MASHED POTATOES (PAGE 136)

1/8 TEASPOON PAPRIKA

1   Preheat oven to 350 degrees.

2   Heat oil in a large cast-iron or oven-safe skillet over medium-high heat. Brown ground beef. Add onion and vegetables and season with onion powder, garlic powder, salt, and pepper.

3   Deglaze the pan with white wine and reduce until wine has evaporated. Mix in tomato paste, Worcestershire sauce, and chicken broth. Bring to a boil over high heat and cook until the sauce has thickened. Allow to cool slightly.

4   Mix cheese in with potatoes and spread over the meat mixture. Sprinkle paprika on top for color. Bake for 30–40 minutes until potatoes are golden.

Make it pretty!

- *Use your fork to create peaks with the mashed potatoes before baking.*

EGG ROLL BOWL

SERVES 4

We all know egg rolls are the MVP of Chinese takeout! With only one pan, and in about 15 minutes, this takes my favorite flavors from the traditional rolls and flips them upside down and inside out! I imagine this would be amazing left over, but we've never had any because the whole family eats it up! Serve as is, over white rice, or even in a lettuce cup.

- 1 TABLESPOON SESAME OIL
- 1 CUP FINELY CHOPPED GREEN ONIONS, PLUS MORE FOR SERVING
- 1 POUND GROUND PORK OR BEEF
- 1/4 TEASPOON SALT
- 1/2 TEASPOON PEPPER
- 2 CLOVES OF GARLIC, MINCED
- 1 BAG (10 OUNCES) SHREDDED CABBAGE OR COLESLAW MIX
- 1 CUP SHREDDED CARROTS
- 1/4 CUP SOY SAUCE
- 2 TABLESPOONS DUCK SAUCE
- 1 TEASPOON GROUND GINGER
- 1 CUP CRISPY WONTON STRIPS

1   Heat sesame oil in a large skillet over medium-heat high heat. Add green onions and ground pork and cook until the meat is no longer pink. Season with salt and pepper. Add garlic and cook for an additional minute.

2   Mix in cabbage, carrots, soy sauce, duck sauce, and ginger. Cook for 5 minutes, tossing frequently, or until vegetables are tender. Top with wonton strips and green onions; season with additional salt and pepper to taste.

Try fresh ginger!

- *Grated fresh ginger packs a flavorful punch for a dish like this. You can pick up a small piece of ginger root in the produce section of your grocery store for a few cents! Start with 2 teaspoons and add more to taste.*

GRANDMA'S GOULASH

All my life I happily ate what my grandma called "goulash." Then I went on a work trip to Budapest, Hungary (home of the actual goulash), and I realized Grandma (as usual) had put her own Italian-American spin on it. Turns out there are tons of goulash variations. Some call it American goulash; here in New England they call it American Chop Suey. Call it whatever you want . . . it's simple, filling, cozy, comfort food at its best.

- 2 CUPS DITALINI PASTA
- 2 TABLESPOONS OLIVE OIL
- 1 SMALL YELLOW ONION, FINELY CHOPPED
- 1 GREEN BELL PEPPER, CORED AND FINELY CHOPPED
- 2 CLOVES OF GARLIC, MINCED
- 1 1/2 POUNDS GROUND BEEF (80/20)
- 2 EGGS
- 1 TEASPOON GARLIC POWDER
- 1 TEASPOON SALT

- 1/2 TEASPOON PEPPER
- 1 CUP FRESHLY GRATED PARMESAN CHEESE, DIVIDED
- 3 TABLESPOONS WORCESTERSHIRE SAUCE
- 1 CAN (14.5 OUNCES) ITALIAN-STYLE DICED TOMATOES, IN THEIR JUICES
- 2 CUPS SPAGHETTI SAUCE (JARRED IS FINE, OR TRY MARIA'S MONDAY MARINARA ON PAGE 45)
- 2 CUPS SHREDDED MOZZARELLA CHEESE (OPTIONAL)

1   Preheat oven to 350 degrees.

2   Cook pasta in salted water according to package instructions for al dente. Drain and set aside.

3   Heat oil in a large Dutch oven over medium-high heat; add onion and pepper and cook until tender. Stir in garlic and cook for another minute. Add ground beef and cook until the meat is no longer pink.

4   In a medium bowl, beat eggs and gradually incorporate into the ground beef. Season with garlic powder, salt, pepper, and half of the Parmesan cheese. Stir in cooked pasta, Worcestershire sauce, diced tomatoes and juices, and spaghetti sauce.

5   Top with remaining Parmesan cheese and mozzarella (if using). Bake for 15 minutes uncovered.

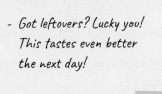

- Got leftovers? Lucky you! This tastes even better the next day!

MA, THE MEATLOAF!

I find meatloaf to be a hilarious food. I mean the very idea of meat in a loaf is just a funny concept. It's been the butt of many jokes and a retro household favorite for as long as I can remember. But, done right, meatloaf is no laughing matter. It's a showstopper! Everyone needs a good meatloaf recipe in their bag of tricks, and this one that originally came from my grandma is mine. My family goes crazy for this, *and* you get bonus points for sneaking in some whole grain oats.

1 1/2 POUNDS GROUND BEEF (80/20)

1 EGG

3/4 CUP WHOLE GRAIN OATS

3/4 CUP FRESHLY GRATED PARMESAN CHEESE

3/4 CUP MILK

1 MEDIUM ONION, FINELY CHOPPED

1 TABLESPOON WORCESTERSHIRE SAUCE

1/2 TEASPOON SALT

1/2 TEASPOON PEPPER

1 BEEF BOUILLON CUBE

1   Preheat oven to 350 degrees.

2   In a large mixing bowl, combine the ground beef, egg, oats, cheese, milk, onion, Worcestershire sauce, salt, and pepper. Gently mix with your hands, combining all ingredients being careful not to overwork the meat.

3   Place the bouillon cube in a 9x13-inch baking dish with a thin layer of water. Form the meat mixture into a loaf smaller than the baking dish, leaving room on each side. Cover with aluminum foil and bake for 1 hour or until it reaches an internal temperature of 160 degrees.

4   Remove foil. Drizzle some of the drippings on top and broil for about 5 minutes or until outside is crispy brown. Allow to cool slightly before slicing and serving.

- Don't undercook. Test your loaf to make sure it's firm. You <u>don't</u> want mushy meatloaf!

- If you like, you can top with a thin layer of ketchup and/or BBQ sauce before putting in the oven.

NOT YOUR SMOTHER'S PAN-FRIED PORK CHOPS

SERVES 4

I could never get my husband to eat pork chops because he said they were "too dry" (and I'd begrudgingly have to agree), but then I started pan frying them and smothering them in homemade gravy. The key is getting bone-in pork chops and not overcooking them. This is one of the quickest recipes in this book and guaranteed to please. This would be great with Parmesan Garlic String Beans (page 139), Old- Fashioned Mashed Potatoes (page 136), or Cabbage Crack (page 131)

PORK CHOPS:

4 MEDIUM-SIZED BONE-IN, PORK LOIN CHOPS (ABOUT 3/4-INCH THICK)

1/2 TEASPOON SALT

1/2 TEASPOON PEPPER

1/2 TEASPOON ONION POWDER

2 TABLESPOONS FLOUR

2 TABLESPOONS OLIVE OIL

1 TABLESPOON BUTTER

GRAVY:

1 TABLESPOON BUTTER

1 LARGE ONION, SLICED INTO THIN RINGS

1 TABLESPOON FLOUR

1 CUP CHICKEN BROTH

1/2 CUP HALF-AND-HALF

1/4 TEASPOON SALT

1/4 TEASPOON PEPPER

1 TEASPOON CHOPPED FRESH PARSLEY, FOR GARNISH

1   Pat pork chops dry. Season each side with salt, pepper, and onion powder then lightly coat with flour. Heat oil and butter in a large cast-iron skillet over medium-high heat. Add pork chops and cook for 3 minutes on each side until golden brown. Remove and let rest.

2   In the same skillet, add butter, onion, and flour; whisk over low heat. Stir in chicken broth, half-and-half, salt, and pepper; continue whisking until thickened.

3   Return pork chops to skillet and cook for another 5 minutes or until they reach an internal temperature of 150–155 degrees. Top with fresh parsley.

- Be sure to get bone-in pork chops. Boneless pork chops aren't as flavorful and could end up dry and tough.

QUICKIE STRIP STEAK
WITH HERB BUTTER

This is the only way I cook my steaks. This impressive dish is simpler than simple. It takes just a few ingredients and is ready in under ten minutes. When it comes to steak, less is more. Top with this fresh herb butter and it will truly melt in your mouth. But fair warning, once you prepare steaks like this at home, you won't be able to overpay at a restaurant for them anymore!

STEAK

1 1/2 POUNDS NEW YORK STRIP STEAK
   (ABOUT 3/4-INCH THICK)
3/4 TEASPOON SALT
1/4 TEASPOON PEPPER

HERB BUTTER:

2 TABLESPOONS SOFTENED, SALTED BUTTER
1/4 TEASPOON GARLIC POWDER
1/2 TEASPOON DRIED ROSEMARY

1   Place an empty cast-iron skillet in the oven. Preheat oven to 500 degrees.

2   Thoroughly pat steak dry with paper towels and generously season with salt and pepper. Set aside.

3   In a small bowl, mix butter, garlic powder, and rosemary; set aside.

4   When the oven temp has reached 500 degrees, carefully remove the very hot skillet and place on the stove over high heat. Add steak to hot, dry skillet and cook 30 seconds without touching to give it a nice brown crust. Flip and cook for another 30 seconds.

5   Carefully put the entire skillet back into the oven. Bake for 3 minutes then flip steak and cook for another 3 minutes for medium-rare. Cook longer to reach desired doneness.

6   Remove the steak from the skillet and set aside. Top with herb butter and let rest for a few minutes before serving.

- Timing is everything. So, get your timer out for this one and be precise! You're not killing a beautiful steak on my watch!

SKILLET STEAK STROGANOFF

SERVES 4

I love a classic beef stroganoff, but it's a low-and-slow kind of dinner and that's not gonna fly for a weeknight. So I came up with something that had all the flavors of this fan favorite in a fraction of the time. In about thirty minutes, this satisfying stroganoff is as luscious as the original thanks to the rich beefy flavors and a lil' boost from the Worcestershire sauce and wine.

12 OUNCES EGG NOODLES

4 TABLESPOONS BUTTER, DIVIDED

1 1/2 POUNDS SIRLOIN STEAK, SLICED INTO 1-INCH CUBES

1/2 TEASPOON SALT, DIVIDED

1/2 TEASPOON PEPPER, DIVIDED

1 MEDIUM ONION, FINELY CHOPPED

1 CLOVE OF GARLIC, MINCED

8 OUNCES SLICED MUSHROOMS

1/4 CUP DRY WHITE WINE

1 TEASPOON WORCESTERSHIRE SAUCE

1/8 TEASPOON GROUND NUTMEG

1 CUP BEEF BROTH

1 TABLESPOON FLOUR

1/4 CUP SOUR CREAM, PLUS MORE FOR SERVING

1/4 CUP CHOPPED FRESH PARSLEY, FOR GARNISH

1   Cook egg noodles according to package instructions. Once drained, toss in 2 tablespoons of butter and season with additional salt and pepper to taste.

2   Season steak pieces with 1/4 teaspoon each salt and pepper.

3   Melt 1 tablespoon of butter in a large cast-iron skillet over medium-high heat. Add steak and cook 2 minutes. Flip and cook for another 2 minutes or until browned on the outside and medium-rare on the inside. Remove and let rest.

4   Add 1 tablespoon of butter to the skillet. Sauté onions and garlic until translucent. Stir in mushrooms, wine, Worcestershire sauce, and nutmeg. Season with remaining salt and pepper. Whisk in beef broth and flour and simmer on low for 3 minutes or until thickened.

5   Remove skillet from heat and blend in sour cream. Return steak to skillet.

6   Serve stroganoff over buttered noodles and top with chopped parsley.

- Marsala is a great substitute if you don't want to use wine.

- For a variation you can use ground sirloin instead of sirloin steak.

STREET-STYLE SAUSAGE & PEPPERS

SERVES 4

As an Italian kid growing up in Erie, Pennsylvania, the annual St Paul's Italian Festival was a big event on the social calendar! The vendors would line up and you couldn't mistake the familiar smell of sausage and peppers! There was bingo for the women, beer for the men, and games for the kids. Every Italian in town was there, so we knew *everybody* and it's such great memories. When I moved to NYC, I absolutely loved hanging out in Little Italy and cruising Mulberry Street seeing diners al fresco on the sidewalk, smelling all the smells, and hearing a bit of Italian in the air. I never missed the San Gennaro Festival where I could feel nostalgic and, of course, get one of those sausage and pepper "sangwiches" (like my Papa used to say)! This skillet meal couldn't be easier! So, add a sausage link and a heaping spoonful of juicy peppers to a buttered hoagie roll and transport yourself to the streets of Little Italy, USA.

1 TABLESPOON OLIVE OIL

1 1/2 POUNDS ITALIAN PORK SAUSAGE
(SWEET AND/OR HOT)

3 BELL PEPPERS, CUT INTO STRIPS

1 LARGE ONION, ROUGHLY CHOPPED

1/4 TEASPOON SALT

1/4 TEASPOON PEPPER

1   Heat olive oil in a large skillet over medium-high heat; add sausage and brown on all sides.

2   Add sliced vegetables to the hot pan and coat in sausage drippings. Reduce heat to medium while tossing occasionally for 5 minutes. Season with salt and pepper.

3   Simmer partially covered and stir occasionally for 30 minutes.

4   Uncover and cook for another 10 minutes or until sausages are cooked through.

- Green peppers are most budget-friendly, and they'll work just fine, but I love to add the color and sweetness of yellow and red ones.

SOUP 'N SALAD

CREAMY TOMATO SOUP

My daughter, Grace, will tell you this is her favorite recipe in the book! This savory, creamy, and just a lil' sweet soup hits all the right spots! Serve with a baked grilled cheese sandwich (page 95) and prepare to lick the bowl clean!

- -

2 TABLESPOONS OLIVE OIL

1 MEDIUM YELLOW ONION, MINCED

3 CLOVES OF GARLIC, MINCED

2 CANS (28 OUNCES EACH) SAN MARZANO
   WHOLE PEELED TOMATOES, IN THEIR
   JUICES

1 CUP WATER

2 TABLESPOONS SUGAR

1 TEASPOON DRIED BASIL

1 TEASPOON SALT

1/2 TEASPOON PEPPER

1 CUP LIGHT CREAM

1/4 CUP CHOPPED FRESH BASIL, PLUS MORE
   FOR GARNISH

1 CUP SHREDDED MOZZARELLA OR FRESHLY
   GRATED PARMESAN CHEESE, DIVIDED

1   Heat olive oil in a large heavy-bottomed soup pot over medium-high heat. Add onions and cook for 2–3 minutes or until translucent. Stir in garlic and cook for an additional minute.

2   Stir in tomatoes and their juices. Mash tomatoes with a wooden spoon or potato masher.

3   Add water, sugar, dried basil, salt, and pepper to the pot. Bring to a boil then reduce heat to a simmer, partially covered, for at least 30 minutes. Remove from heat and stir in cream.

- **IF YOU LIKE A SMOOTHER SOUP:** use an immersion blender, or transfer to a regular blender in portions, and puree until smooth.

- **IF YOU LIKE A CHUNKIER SOUP:** puree only half of the mixture.

4   Stir in fresh basil. Season with additional salt and pepper to taste. Top with cheese and garnish with more fresh basil.

Time saver!

- Pour sugar in a salt shaker or an empty spice container and keep it close so it's easily accessible for dishes like this

EASY CHEESY
BROCCOLI SOUP

SERVES 6-8

At the risk of sounding cheesy, I must say, this one is *special*. When I was little, Grandma Grace would take me to this teeny tiny diner called Kathleen's. Grandma was old-school and didn't drive, so we'd walk, and by the time we arrived, I was famished. There wasn't much on the menu, but all you need is one gem, and Kathleen's Cheese Broccoli Soup was hers. I'll never know exactly how she made it, but I tested this one to pieces until I got it right. This is comfort food all the way. Kids just love it, and for this big kid, it takes me back to the good ol' days and a very special treat with Grandma.

4 TABLESPOONS BUTTER

1 MEDIUM YELLOW ONION, FINELY CHOPPED

1 CUP SHREDDED CARROT

1 CUP FINELY CHOPPED CELERY

1/2 TEASPOON SALT

1/2 TEASPOON PEPPER

1 CLOVE OF GARLIC, MINCED

2 TABLESPOONS FLOUR

2 CUPS CHICKEN STOCK

1 BAG (16 OUNCES) FROZEN CHOPPED BROCCOLI, THAWED

2 CUPS HALF-AND-HALF

2 CUPS SHREDDED CHEDDAR CHEESE, PLUS MORE FOR SERVING

1   Heat butter in a large heavy-bottomed soup pot over medium heat until melted, being careful not to burn. Stir in onions, carrots, and celery. Season with salt and pepper and cook 10 minutes or until tender. Add garlic and sauté for another minute.

2   Sprinkle flour over vegetables and toss to coat. Cook for one minute. Pour in chicken stock and whisk until thickened, then add broccoli. Reduce heat to low, cover, and simmer about 15 minutes or until broccoli is tender. Stir occasionally so it doesn't stick to the bottom of the pot.

3   Slowly stir in half-and-half. Add cheese a bit at a time. Keep stirring until cheese has completely melted. Season with additional salt and pepper to taste. Top with additional shredded cheese when serving.

- If the soup gets too thick, add a 1/4-1/2 cup of chicken stock until it's the consistency you like.

EMBARRASSINGLY EASY CHILI

SERVES 6-8

Ready for the world's easiest chili recipe? I got it from my mama! And it's so easy it's *practically* embarrassing! With only five ingredients and one pot, this has been my weeknight go-to for as long as I've been cooking. There are a million ways to make chili, but as my mom taught me long ago, this is the quick and easy way to get there. This dish is perfect on its own, but who doesn't love a great accessory? Feel free to dress it up with hot sauce, sour cream, cilantro, green onions, shredded cheddar, or crunchy corn chips.

2 TABLESPOONS OLIVE OIL

1 1/2 POUNDS GROUND BEEF (80/20)

1 TABLESPOON CHILI POWDER, DIVIDED

1/2 TEASPOON SALT

1/2 TEASPOON PEPPER

2 CUPS V8 JUICE

2 CANS (14.5 OUNCES EACH) KIDNEY BEANS AND/OR BLACK BEANS, DRAINED AND RINSED

1 CAN (14.5 OUNCES) ITALIAN-STYLE STEWED TOMATOES, IN THEIR JUICES

1 CAN (14.5 OUNCE) CORN, DRAINED

1   Heat oil in a large Dutch oven or stock pot over medium-high heat. Add ground beef and cook until browned, making sure to break up the meat. Drain some of the fat. Season with 1/2 tablespoon chili powder, salt, and pepper.

2   In the same pot, add V8, beans, tomatoes, corn, and remaining chili powder; stir well. Bring to a boil then reduce to a simmer, uncovered, for at least 45 minutes or until the chili reaches desired thickness. Season with additional salt and pepper to taste.

- The simple way to drain fat: Move beef to one side of the pot and soak up the desired amount of grease with a paper towel.

- Party ideas: Scoop chili into a bag of corn chips, add it to a hot dog, or scoop it on top of nachos or a hot baked potato.

KALE YEAH SALAD
WITH GOLDEN GARLIC
CROUTONS

SERVES 4-6

If you think kale is boring, I say, "Oh, kale NO!" Living in LA (the unofficial kale capital of the world), I hopped right on the kale train. I used to say we "moved to LA for the weather, stayed for the kale." That was a joke. We stayed for the avocados. Anyway, this has both AND goat cheese. And when it comes to cheeses, they don't call it the G.O.A.T. (Greatest of All Time) for nothing!

GOLDEN GARLIC CROUTONS:

1 TABLESPOON OLIVE OIL

1 TEASPOON GARLIC POWDER

1/4 TEASPOON SALT

4 CUPS FRENCH BREAD, CUT INTO 1-INCH
    CUBES

SALAD:

12 OUNCES KALE, ROUGHLY CHOPPED

1/2 CUP PREPARED BALSAMIC VINAIGRETTE

3/4 CUP CRUMBLED GOAT CHEESE

1 SMALL RED ONION, THINLY SLICED

1 RIPE AVOCADO, SLICED

1 CUP HALVED CHERRY TOMATOES

1 CUCUMBER, DICED

1 CUP SLICED ALMONDS

1   Preheat oven to 400 degrees.

2   In a large mixing bowl, combine olive oil, garlic powder, and salt. Add cubed bread and toss to coat. Spread onto a baking sheet and bake for 5 minutes. Remove from oven, flip croutons, and continue baking for an additional 5 minutes or until golden brown.

3   In the same large mixing bowl, add kale, vinaigrette, croutons, and remaining ingredients. Toss well. Season with additional salt and pepper to taste.

- Throw in leftovers! This would be great with roasted sweet potatoes, Brussels sprouts, corn, or rice. I love a warm element to a salad.

INSTANT RAMEN REVAMP

This was inspired by the best meal I ever had! Picture it . . . a very rainy day in Tokyo, Japan. I was twenty-something years old and on the work trip of a lifetime! My TV crew and I had been busy shooting all over Japan. We were cold, soaking wet, and (if I'm being real) slightly hungover from last night's sake, and we were starved. Low and behold, we stumble upon a ramen shop. We duck out of the rain, head down a dark flight of stairs, and find ourselves in the coziest little restaurant. The waiter brings over piping hot ramen, a bowl of pickles, and a mug of cold beer. All the conditions were right—and it was the best meal I ever had! Now, this recipe is not that. It couldn't possibly be. But there are countless ways to upgrade your instant ramen. Top with hot sauce and serve with a bowl of pickles and a cold beer (Tokyo style).

1 TABLESPOON SALTED BUTTER

1 CLOVE OF GARLIC, MINCED

1 TABLESPOON FRESH GRATED GINGER

3 CUPS SLICED SHIITAKE MUSHROOMS

1 TABLESPOON SOY SAUCE

1/2 TEASPOON PEPPER

8 CUPS CHICKEN BROTH, DIVIDED

1 CUP WATER

1 EGG

3 CUPS CHOPPED BOK CHOY

2 PACKAGES (3 OUNCES EACH) RAMEN NOODLES, SEASONING PACKET DISCARDED

1 CUP COOKED CHICKEN, PORK, OR TOFU (OPTIONAL)

1/2 CUP FINELY SLICED GREEN ONIONS

1. Heat butter in a large heavy-bottomed soup pot over medium heat. Add garlic and ginger and sauté for 1 minute. Stir in mushrooms, soy sauce, pepper, and 1 cup of chicken broth. Cook for 5 minutes or until mushrooms are tender. Pour in the remaining chicken broth and water and bring to a boil.

2. In a small bowl, whisk the egg. Slowly add the whisked egg to the heated soup while gently stirring. Add bok choy and noodles and cook until noodles are tender. Mix in cooked protein, if desired. Garnish with fresh green onions.

- I'm clearly no MD, but I swear this has medicinal capabilities! When you're feeling run down, had too much fun last night, or just need to warm up on a cold day, a piping hot bowl of ramen is just what the doctor ordered.

ITALIAN CHICKEN STEW

SERVES 4-6

Rustic, hearty, and full of flavor, this is the perfect dish on a crisp day. Grandma called this chicken cacciatore, but I think it's better described as chicken stew with an Italian twist. Serve with crusty bread or over rice.

2 TABLESPOONS OLIVE OIL

2 POUNDS BONELESS, SKINLESS CHICKEN THIGHS

1/2 TEASPOON SALT

1/2 TEASPOON PEPPER

1 MEDIUM ONION, FINELY CHOPPED

2 CLOVES OF GARLIC, MINCED

3 CANS (14.5 OUNCES EACH) ITALIAN-STYLE STEWED TOMATOES

1 CUP WATER

1 CHICKEN BOUILLON CUBE

1/2 TEASPOON DRIED BASIL

2 LARGE POTATOES, PEELED AND CUT INTO 1/2-INCH CUBES

1 RED BELL PEPPER, DICED

1 CAN (14.5 OUNCES) PEAS, DRAINED AND RINSED

1   Heat oil in a large heavy-bottomed pot over medium-high heat. Season chicken with salt and pepper and brown on both sides for 3–5 minutes. Add onions and cook until translucent. Stir in garlic and cook for an additional minute.

2   Stir in tomatoes, water, bouillon cube, basil, potatoes, and bell pepper. Simmer, uncovered, for 30 minutes or until potatoes are tender and sauce has thickened. Add peas and cook until heated through. Season with additional salt and pepper to taste.

TUSCAN VEGETABLE BEAN SOUP

SERVES 6-8

Oh $#!%, you bought too much produce! I can't tell you how many times my eyes were bigger than my stomach at the farmers market. If you're not actually the person you thought you were when you bought all those veggies and they're just staring at you every time you open the fridge, then this is for you! I was originally introduced to this hearty soup when I was a student living in Florence, Italy, and it was love at first bite.

1/4 CUP OLIVE OIL, PLUS MORE FOR SERVING

1 LARGE ONION, DICED

1 CLOVE OF GARLIC, MINCED

1 CUP DICED CARROT

1 LARGE BUNCH SWISS CHARD, WASHED, STEMMED, AND ROUGHLY CHOPPED

1 LARGE POTATO (SKIN ON), CHOPPED INTO BITE-SIZE PIECES

2 CUPS ZUCCHINI, CHOPPED INTO BITE-SIZE PIECES

1 CAN (14.5 OUNCES) STEWED OR DICED TOMATOES, IN THEIR JUICES

2 CUPS WATER

PARMESAN CHEESE RIND, 1-INCH

1/2 TEASPOON SALT

1/4 TEASPOON PEPPER

1 CAN (14.5 OUNCES) CANNELLINI BEANS, RINSED AND DRAINED

FRESHLY GRATED PARMESAN CHEESE, FOR SERVING

1   Heat olive oil in a large soup pot over high heat. Add onions and sauté for 5 minutes or until tender. Toss in garlic and continue cooking for another minute.

2   Stir in remaining vegetables, water, Parmesan rind, salt, and pepper; simmer partially uncovered over medium heat for 20–30 minutes or until vegetables are tender. Fold in half of the beans.

3   Mash or puree the remaining beans and then add to the soup. Cook until heated through. Season with additional salt and pepper to taste.

4   Top with a drizzle of olive oil and grated cheese.

- Don't toss those cheese rinds. They are packed full of flavor and come in handy for soups like this or to toss into a pot of spaghetti sauce.

WEEKNIGHT WEDDING SOUP

My dad is famous for his wedding soup. It's amazing, but he makes it an all-day ordeal. Now, don't get me wrong, making your own broth and mini meatballs is great, but NOT on a Tuesday night. So, he and I worked together to make his laborious wedding soup simple enough for a weeknight. With a little help from some store-bought ingredients, this takes a fraction of the time and does not miss a beat. Dad says, "It couldn't be any better." And let me tell you, he's a tough customer.

- -

8 CUPS CHICKEN BROTH

1 CUP WATER

1 POUND BONELESS, SKINLESS CHICKEN BREAST

1 POUND FROZEN MINI-MEATBALLS OR HOMEMADE (PAGE 53)

3 CARROTS, PEELED AND CHOPPED

3 CELERY STALKS, CHOPPED

1 MEDIUM YELLOW ONION, HALVED

1/2 TEASPOON BLACK PEPPER

1 CUP UNCOOKED ORZO PASTA

2 CUPS CHOPPED FRESH SPINACH

2 EGGS

1/2 CUP FRESHLY GRATED PARMESAN CHEESE, PLUS MORE FOR SERVING

1   In a large stock pot, add chicken broth, water, chicken, meatballs, carrots, celery, onion, and pepper; bring to a boil. (Don't bother chopping the onion. It will be removed before serving.) Boil for 30 minutes or until chicken is cooked through and no longer pink.

2   Remove one ladle of broth and set aside to cool. (You'll use this in a few minutes.)

3   Remove chicken and shred with a fork. Return shredded chicken to the pot and reduce heat to a simmer. Add uncooked pasta and chopped spinach.

4   Meanwhile, crack eggs into a small bowl and gently whisk. Add the Parmesan cheese and the cool broth to your egg mixture. (If it's too hot, it will scramble the egg.) Slowly add the egg mixture to the soup while stirring constantly. Remove the onion.

5   Serve with additional grated cheese for the table.

Chicken broth versus chicken stock:

- *Chicken broth has more salt and therefore more flavor. If you only have chicken stock or prefer to control the amount of salt you use in your soup, just add one chicken bouillon cube for flavor or salt to taste.*

THE WEDGE
WITH AUNT RAY'S BLUE CHEESE DRESSING

SERVES 4

I cannot pass up a wedge salad, but it was always one of those treats reserved for when we were out to dinner. But why? It's time to bring the steakhouse home! Top it with Aunt Ray's famous blue cheese dressing and you've got yourself a decadent treat! My great-aunt made dressing so delicious she bottled it up and started a successful salad dressing company. She sold the business and with it all of the recipes, but one was just too good to let go. Years ago, the famous blue cheese dressing was passed down to my Aunt Raylene and has remained a family secret . . . until now.

THE WEDGE:

1/2 POUND SLICED BACON

1 HEAD ICEBERG LETTUCE

1 CUP HALVED CHERRY TOMATOES

1/2 SMALL RED ONION, THINLY SLICED

AUNT RAY'S BLUE CHEESE DRESSING:

1 TEASPOON DRY MUSTARD

1 TEASPOON SALT

1/4 TEASPOON BLACK PEPPER

4 OUNCES CREAM CHEESE, SOFTENED

1/3 CUP APPLE CIDER VINEGAR

1 CUP VEGETABLE OIL

1 CUP CRUMBLED BLUE CHEESE

1. Preheat oven to 425 degrees.

2. Arrange bacon on an aluminum foil–covered baking sheet. Bake in the oven for 15–20 minutes or until crispy brown. Remove and set aside on paper towels to absorb the grease.

3. Meanwhile, in a medium mixing bowl, combine mustard, salt, and pepper. Add softened cream cheese and mix well until blended. Gradually whisk in vinegar. Slowly add the oil, whisking vigorously as you go. Fold in crumbled blue cheese, and mix well.

4. Cut lettuce into quarters for a traditional wedge or roughly chop and serve in a large mixing bowl. Top with crumbled crispy bacon and tomatoes. Drizzle blue cheese dressing over salad and enjoy.

Pro Tip!

- *Soak sliced red onion for 10 minutes in cold water before adding to salads to mellow its sharp flavor.*

SAMMIES 'N STUFF

BAKED GRILLED CHEESE

You may be thinking, c'mon now . . . I don't really need a recipe for grilled cheese! How hard can it be? But with this baking technique, you can make enough sandwiches to feed the whole neighborhood all at once. No more standing over the hot stove flipping sandwiches one at a time. Every bite will be perfectly cooked to crunchy, oozy, cheesy perfection.

2 TABLESPOONS OLIVE OIL

2 TABLESPOONS BUTTER

8 LARGE SLICES SOURDOUGH BREAD

8-12 SLICES PROVOLONE CHEESE

1   Preheat oven to 450 degrees.

2   Spread olive oil on a large sheet pan. Butter one side of each bread slice.

3   Place four slices of bread, butter-side down, on the prepared pan. Top with 2–3 slices of cheese. Top with the remaining slices of bread, butter-side up.

4   Bake for 6 minutes. Flip and bake for another 6 minutes or until golden brown.

BINGO BURGERS

Smash burgers are all the rage, but I've been eating these my whole life! With the smashing approach, you cook your burger in its own juices on a very hot surface, which gives the patties a crispy crust, juicy insides, and intense flavor. Lovingly called the Bingo Burger because my grandma made these every Monday night so she could quickly get dinner on the table and head out the door in time to get her seat at BINGO! Serve as is or pile high with lettuce, tomato, onion, and pickle.

1 POUND GROUND BEEF (80/20)

1 TEASPOON SALT

1/2 TEASPOON PEPPER

1 TABLESPOON VEGETABLE OIL

1 TABLESPOON BUTTER, PLUS MORE FOR BUTTERING BUN

4 SLICES AMERICAN CHEESE

4 HAMBURGER BUNS

1   Divide ground beef into four sections and season each with salt and pepper. No need to form into patties.

2   Heat vegetable oil and butter in a large skillet or griddle over medium-high heat until butter is melted. Place patties in the hot pan, smash down with a spatula, and cook for about 2 minutes. Leave them alone! Flip, smash, and cook for another 3-4 minutes until edges are crispy and meat is cooked through. Add a slice of cheese to each burger and cook until melted. Remove from the pan.

3   Generously butter the inside of the buns and place butter-side down on the hot pan until toasted. Add your beef patties and toppings of choice.

- Plan on at least 1/4-pound patty per person, so adjust the recipe as needed for your crew.

BLT AVOCADO TOAST

A BLT or avocado toast is always my weekend brunch order, so I figured let's marry them! And while we're at it, why wait for the weekend? Let's face it—the smell of bacon wafting through the house on a weeknight just hits different!

1 POUND SLICED BACON

2 TABLESPOONS OLIVE OIL, DIVIDED

8 SLICES SOURDOUGH BREAD

8 LARGE, GREEN LEAF LETTUCE LEAVES

1 LARGE TOMATO, SLICED INTO ROUNDS

AVOCADO SPREAD:

2 LARGE RIPE AVOCADOS

1 TABLESPOON OLIVE OIL

2 TABLESPOONS FRESH LEMON JUICE

1/4 TEASPOON ONION POWDER

1/4 TEASPOON SALT

1/4 TEASPOON PEPPER

1. Preheat oven to 425 degrees.

2. Arrange bacon on an aluminum foil–covered sheet pan. Bake in the oven for 15–20 minutes or until crispy brown.

3. Drizzle 1 tablespoon of olive oil on another sheet pan. Arrange bread in a single layer and brush with remaining tablespoon of olive oil. Bake for 3–4 minutes or until lightly toasted. Remove from the oven.

4. Meanwhile, mash avocado in a medium bowl. Mix in olive oil, lemon juice, onion powder, salt, and pepper; stir until combined.

5. Spread the mashed avocado over toasted bread and top with bacon, lettuce, and tomato.

- Baking bacon is truly the only way to go! Easy cleanup and cooked just the way you like it every single time.

PAPA'S PIZZA

In my family, we like to say, "all pizza is good, some is just better than others." This recipe is passed down from my dad, who considers making pizza, eating pizza, and pizza in general his hobby—so you know it's good. We've been making this every Friday for as long as I can remember. It's so fun to prepare as a family and even quicker than delivery!

1 PACKAGE (16 OUNCES) STORE-BOUGHT PIZZA DOUGH

1 TABLESPOON OLIVE OIL

1 TABLESPOON FLOUR

1 1/2 CUPS PIZZA SAUCE (PAGE 103)

1/4 TEASPOON GRANULATED GARLIC

1/4 CUP FRESHLY GRATED PARMESAN CHEESE

1 CUP SHREDDED MOZZARELLA CHEESE

2-INCH PEPPERONI STICK, THINLY SLICED

1 Remove dough from original packaging; place on a plate and cover tightly with plastic wrap to prevent drying. Rest at room temp for about 1 hour until it rises slightly and is pillow-soft.

2 Preheat oven to 475 degrees.

3 Lightly oil a 14-inch pizza pan or 10x14-inch baking sheet with olive oil.

4 Dust the outside of the dough ball with flour. Using your hands, take your time to gently stretch the dough until it's thin but not tearing. You may use a rolling pin to get it to desired size. Place dough on the pan and stretch to the outer edges of the pan.

5 Ladle sauce evenly over the dough, leaving a border around the edges. Top with granulated garlic, Parmesan cheese, mozzarella cheese, and pepperoni.

6 Bake for 15 minutes or until the crust is golden brown and crisp but not burnt.

7 Slide the pizzas onto a pizza peel or cutting board to cool. Slice and *mangia* ("eat up")!!!

- Use the pepperoni that comes in a stick so it will "cup and char." (In other words, curl up and hold onto that yummy pepperoni grease.)

- Add more toppings! Pile high with mushroom, peppers, sausage, or just about anything (except pineapple . . . please NO pineapple).

NO-COOK PIZZA SAUCE

MAKES 3 1/2 CUPS

The best pizza I ever had was (obviously!) in Italy. When I studied abroad in Italy, the locals said the further south you get, the better the pizza gets. So, in the name of pizza research, I took what little money I had and hopped a train to Naples, home of the original margherita pizza. Let me tell you, it was everything they said it would be and more! Absolute pizza perfection! Now clearly, we're not in Italy and we don't have all those fresh ingredients at our fingertips, but with just a few ingredients, you can whip up a simple, no-cook sauce the Italian way.

1 CAN (28 OUNCES) WHOLE PEELED SAN MARZANO TOMATOES, IN THEIR JUICES

2 TABLESPOONS OLIVE OIL

2 CLOVES OF GARLIC, MINCED

1 TEASPOON FINELY CHOPPED FRESH BASIL

1 TEASPOON DRIED OREGANO

1 TEASPOON SUGAR

1/2 TEASPOON SALT

1/4 TEASPOON PEPPER

1   Place tomatoes and their juices in a large bowl and use your hands to mash. Stir in all other ingredients and mix well.

SLOPPY GIUSEPPES

There is something so playful and fun about a good ol' sloppy Joe. Granted, my family called them Sloppy Giuseppes in keeping with the theme of making even non-Italian things Italian. Whatever you call it, it's on the table in about a half hour and there's never a morsel left over!

- -

1 TABLESPOON OLIVE OIL

1 1/2 POUNDS GROUND BEEF (80/20)

1 TEASPOON SALT

1/2 TEASPOON PEPPER

1 MEDIUM YELLOW ONION, DICED

1 GREEN BELL PEPPER, DICED

2 CLOVES OF GARLIC, MINCED

1/4 CUP KETCHUP

1/4 CUP BBQ SAUCE

2 TEASPOONS WORCESTERSHIRE SAUCE

1 TEASPOON DRY MUSTARD

1 TEASPOON GARLIC POWDER

4 SESAME HAMBURGER BUNS OR KAISER ROLLS

1 TABLESPOON BUTTER

2 DILL PICKLES, SLICED INTO ROUNDS

1. Heat olive oil in a large skillet over medium-high heat. Add beef, season with salt and pepper, and cook until browned. Drain some of the fat.

2. Toss in onions and bell pepper; cook until onions are translucent. Add garlic and cook for another minute.

3. Reduce heat to low and stir in ketchup, BBQ sauce, Worcestershire sauce, dry mustard, and garlic powder. Simmer for 15 minutes. Season with additional salt and pepper to taste.

4. Butter the inside of the buns and place on a hot griddle or pan to toast.

5. Spoon the Joe mix onto the toasted buns, top with pickles, and serve with crunchy potato chips.

- If you prefer it sloppier, just add more ketchup and BBQ sauce!

- Load on sliced cheese and make it a sloppy melt!

HOT MESS ITALIAN HOAGIE
WITH CHOPPED PEPPER SALAD

SERVES 4

There are few sandwiches on this planet that I enjoy more than an Italian combination sub. At least that's what we called it where I grew up in Erie, Pennsylvania. Overstuffed and spicy, this one is a hot mess in all the right ways! It's a winning combo of Italian cold cuts topped with melted cheese and piled high with homemade chopped pepper salad. Feel free to add some hot peppers, or "hots," to give it an extra kick!

1 LARGE LOAF ITALIAN BREAD

1/4 POUND THINLY SLICED MORTADELLA (ITALIAN BOLOGNA)

1/4 POUND THINLY SLICED SANDWICH PEPPERONI

1/4 POUND THINLY SLICED GENOA SALAMI

1/4 POUND THINLY SLICED HAM OR CAPICOLA (ITALIAN HOT HAM)

1/4 POUND THINLY SLICED MOZZARELLA CHEESE

1/4 POUND THINLY SLICED PROVOLONE CHEESE

2 CUPS FINELY CHOPPED ICEBERG LETTUCE

1 CUP DICED RED ONION

1 CUP CHOPPED BANANA PEPPER RINGS OR HOT PEPPERS

1 CUP CHOPPED PICKLES

1/2 CUP ITALIAN DRESSING, PLUS MORE FOR SERVING

1/2 BEEFSTEAK TOMATO, THINLY SLICED

1   Preheat oven to 375 degrees.

2   Slice the loaf of bread horizontally to create a giant sandwich. Layer meats and cheeses.

3   Bake open-faced for 10–15 minutes or until the meat is warm throughout and the cheese has melted.

4   Meanwhile, in a large bowl, combine lettuce, onion, peppers, and pickles. Toss with Italian dressing.

5   Remove the sandwich from the oven. Top with sliced tomato and pepper salad. Fold and cut into pieces.

STROMBOLI

Not sandwich, or pizza, or even its cousin the calzone. The stromboli, my friends, is in a league of its own. In our house, this was reserved for special occasions, but because it's so easy to make and Y.O.L.O (you only live once!) . . . I say why wait for a holiday?

- -

1 PACKAGE (16 OUNCES) STORE-BOUGHT
   PIZZA DOUGH

2 TABLESPOONS OLIVE OIL, DIVIDED

1/3 POUND SLICED SALAMI

1/4 POUND SLICED PROVOLONE CHEESE

1/3 POUND SLICED SANDWICH PEPPERONI

1/4 POUND SLICED MOZZARELLA CHEESE

1 TEASPOON GRANULATED GARLIC

1 TABLESPOON ITALIAN-STYLE BREAD
   CRUMBS

1. Remove dough from original packaging; place on a plate and cover tightly with plastic wrap to prevent drying. Rest at room temp for about 1 hour until it rises slightly and is pillow-soft.

2. Preheat oven to 400 degrees. Grease a 13x18-inch baking sheet with 1 tablespoon olive oil.

3. Stretch dough to create a rectangle (it should almost reach the edges).

4. In the center of the dough, layer salami and provolone. Fold over one side of the dough to cover the meat. Now layer pepperoni and mozzarella on top of the dough you just folded over. Stretch the remaining dough over the meat, fold over, and pinch all of the edges.

5. Brush another tablespoon of olive oil on top of dough. Season with granulated garlic and bread crumbs. Cut five 1-inch slits into the top of the dough to vent.

6. Bake uncovered for 20–25 minutes or until golden on top and bottom.

7. Allow to cool slightly, slice into 1-inch pieces, and serve alone or with a side of marinara sauce.

- If dough becomes too sticky to work with, lightly dust with flour.

THE JOSH

You may see it in some delis or diners called "The Rachel," but around here, it's known as "The Josh." This is my husband's all-time favorite, and because he put up with the maniac in me as I wrote this cookbook, the least I can do is give the guy a sandwich! It's a delicious turkey and cheese melt piled high with homemade pickled coleslaw. Serve with pickles and potato chips.

- 2 TABLESPOONS OLIVE OIL
- 2 TABLESPOONS BUTTER
- 8 SLICES JEWISH RYE BREAD
- 1 POUND THINLY SLICED DELI TURKEY BREAST
- 8 SLICES SWISS CHEESE
- 1/2 CUP RUSSIAN DRESSING
- 2 CUPS PICKLED SLAW (PAGE 140)

1. Preheat oven to 425 degrees.

2. Grease a baking sheet with olive oil. Butter one side of each bread slice and place butter-side down. Layer half of the slices with turkey and cheese; bake 10 minutes or until cheese has melted and sandwich is warm throughout. Remove from the oven.

3. Drizzle with Russian dressing and a heaping pile of pickled slaw. Top with another slice of toasted bread.

MEATLESS
MONDAY

ANYTHING GOES VEGGIE FRITTATA

Who doesn't love breakfast for dinner? This frittata is perfect in a pinch and a great way to use up leftovers. Seriously anything goes, but here are a few ideas: try chopped asparagus, peas, and fennel or bell peppers, zucchini, and tomatoes or mushroom, potato, and kale. The combinations are endless!

3 TABLESPOONS OLIVE OIL

1 SMALL ONION, FINELY CHOPPED

2 CUPS CHOPPED VEGETABLES OF YOUR CHOICE

3/4 TEASPOON SALT, DIVIDED

1/4 TEASPOON PEPPER, DIVIDED

8 EGGS

1 CUP SHREDDED OR CRUMBLED CHEESE (LIKE CHEDDAR, GRUYÈRE, FETA, GOAT CHEESE), DIVIDED

1   Preheat oven to 375 degrees.

2   Heat oil in a 10-inch cast-iron skillet or oven-safe frying pan over medium-high heat. Sauté onions and chopped vegetables, season with half the salt and pepper, and cook for 10 minutes or until tender.

3   In a large bowl, beat eggs then fold in 1/2 cup of cheese and remaining salt and pepper.

4   Pour egg mixture into skillet and cook over medium heat for 5 minutes, allowing eggs to set up. Top with remaining cheese.

5   Transfer to the oven and cook for another 10 minutes or until eggs are cooked through.

6   Season with additional salt and pepper to taste.

GIANT LOADED LATKE

It's a potato pancake but family style! Potato pancakes were in the regular rotation at Grandma's house because my grandparents didn't eat meat on Fridays. She usually served them with cottage cheese and applesauce, which always hit the spot. Then cut to my adult life—I married into a big, fabulous Jewish family where I was introduced to "latkes" . . . an old familiar friend with a new name! I like to make one giant latke to save on time, and the kids love to pick it up like a pizza. Feel free to load it up with additional toppings and slice into individual triangles for serving.

2 POUNDS RUSSET POTATOES (ABOUT 2 LARGE POTATOES)

1 MEDIUM YELLOW ONION, QUARTERED

1 TEASPOON SALT

1/4 TEASPOON BLACK PEPPER

2 EGGS

1/2 CUP BREAD CRUMBS

4 TABLESPOONS VEGETABLE OIL, FOR FRYING

1/4 CUP FINELY CHOPPED GREEN ONIONS

SOUR CREAM, FOR SERVING (OPTIONAL)

1 Preheat oven to 425 degrees.

2 In a food processor fitted with the grating attachment, grate potatoes and onions. Drain excess water from the grated mixture and then transfer to a kitchen towel or nut bag and squeeze out as much liquid as possible.

3 Add the mixture to a large mixing bowl and season with salt and pepper. Fold in eggs and bread crumbs a bit at a time.

4 Heat oil in a 12-inch cast-iron skillet or oven-safe frying pan over medium-high heat. Pour in potato mixture and press down with a spatula, forming one large flat pancake. Fry until golden brown on the bottom.

5 Transfer into the oven and bake for 15 minutes or until golden brown and crispy on top.

6 Flip latke onto a serving plate. Top with green onions and a dollop of sour cream if desired.

- If you don't have a food processor, grate the potatoes and onions on the large holes of a box grater, or if you really want to save on time, buy the pre-shredded potatoes in the freezer section of your grocery store.

BIG A$$ SHEET PAN QUESADILLA

Sauté 'em if you got 'em! Use any veggies you've got in the fridge, stuff them all into a giant quesadilla, bake it in the oven, and save yourself the aggravation of cooking them one at a time. This will feed the entire family all at once, and baking it this way makes every bite nice and crispy. Serve with extra salsa, sour cream, hot sauce, and any other toppings you like.

- 2 TABLESPOONS OLIVE OIL
- 1 LARGE RED ONION, THINLY SLICED INTO ROUNDS
- 1 MEDIUM ZUCCHINI, SLICED INTO 1/4-INCH ROUNDS
- 1 MEDIUM YELLOW SQUASH, SLICED INTO 1/4-INCH ROUNDS
- 1 CUP SLICED MUSHROOMS

- 3 CUPS FRESH SPINACH
- 1/2 TEASPOON SALT
- 1/2 TEASPOON PEPPER
- 1/2 CUP SALSA, PLUS MORE FOR SERVING
- 8 BURRITO-SIZE FLOUR TORTILLAS
- 2 CUPS SHREDDED MEXICAN BLEND CHEESE
- 1 TABLESPOON BUTTER

1. Preheat oven to 400 degrees.

2. Heat olive oil in a large skillet over medium-high heat. Add veggies, salt, pepper and salsa and sauté for 10 minutes or until vegetables tender.

3. Meanwhile, spray cooking spray on an 18x13-inch baking sheet. Layer six tortillas around the baking sheet so that the bottom is covered and a bit of each tortilla hangs over the edge.

4. Using tongs, remove veggies from pan and arrange on top of tortillas. Add cheese.

5. Now, fold the overhanging tortillas toward the center of the baking sheet (like you're wrapping a present) and place the remaining two tortillas on top so that none of the mixture shows through.

6. Place a second 18x13-inch baking sheet on top of the quesadilla and bake for 15 minutes. Remove the top baking sheet and spread butter on top of tortillas. Return, uncovered, to the oven and continue baking for another 10 minutes.

7. Slice into rectangles using a pizza cutter.

- If you have picky eaters, you can customize the filling in quadrants so everyone gets exactly what they want!

MAMA'S STOVETOP MAC & CHEESE

Forget the boxed stuff! In the same amount of time, you can whip up this decadent homemade mac and cheese on the stovetop. This is the perfect "in a pinch kind" of meal. And of course, the kids love it . . . because, you know . . . it's macaroni and cheese. I lost track of how many times I tested this! One, because it's awesome, and two, if I was going to include a mac and cheese recipe in this book, it better damn well be a good one! Well, it is.

1 POUND MACARONI, ELBOWS, OR SMALL SHELLS

4 TABLESPOONS BUTTER

2 TABLESPOONS FLOUR

2 CUPS MILK

1 CUP SOUR CREAM

1 TEASPOON SALT

1/2 TEASPOON PEPPER

1 TEASPOON GROUND MUSTARD

3 CUPS SHREDDED SHARP CHEDDAR CHEESE

1   Cook pasta according to package instructions for al dente, but don't drain.

2   Meanwhile, melt butter in a large pot over medium-high heat. Reduce heat to low and sprinkle in flour, stirring continuously. Gradually pour milk into the mixture while whisking constantly; simmer for several minutes or until thickened.

3   Stir in sour cream, salt, pepper, and ground mustard. Fold in cheese a little bit at a time.

4   Using a slotted spoon, add pasta to the cheese mixture. (This is important because that little bit of starchy pasta water will make the sauce silky.) Gently stir to combine. Season with additional salt and pepper to taste. Serve immediately.

- If your kids will allow it, throw in some cooked veggies—like peas or broccoli—after you add the milk.

ITALIAN-STYLE MAC & CHEESE

SERVES 6

I've been accused of making everything Italian style. I just can't help myself! My grandma made her mac and cheese like this, and I think it's a nice twist.

- 1 TABLESPOON OLIVE OIL
- 1 SMALL ONION, CHOPPED
- 1 TABLESPOON GARLIC, MINCED
- 1 CAN (14.5 OUNCES) ITALIAN-STYLE STEWED TOMATOES
- 1 TEASPOON DRIED OREGANO
- 1 TEASPOON SALT
- 1 TEASPOON PEPPER

- STOVETOP CREAMY MAC & CHEESE (PAGE 121), MADE WITH A MIX OF ITALIAN CHEESES (LIKE MOZZARELLA, FONTINA, ASIAGO, AND/OR FRESHLY GRATED PARMESAN) INSTEAD OF CHEDDAR
- 1/2 CUP FRESHLY GRATED PARMESAN CHEESE
- 1/2 CUP ITALIAN-STYLE BREAD CRUMBS

1. Heat olive oil in a pot. Add onion, garlic, tomatoes, oregano, salt, and pepper; simmer uncovered for 15 minutes or until juices have reduced.

2. Transfer macaroni and cheese to casserole dish. Layer tomato sauce on top, along with more Parmesan cheese and bread crumbs. Broil for 5 minutes or until bread crumbs are browned.

VEGGIE FRIED RICE

There's something about this classic Chinese comfort food that is just so satisfying. The whole family loves it, and it's a great way to get my kids to eat some veggies!

2 TABLESPOON VEGETABLE OIL

1 MEDIUM WHITE ONION, FINELY CHOPPED

2 CLOVES OF GARLIC, MINCED

1 BAG (16 OUNCES) FROZEN VEGETABLE MIX, THAWED

1 TABLESPOON SESAME OIL

1/4 CUP SOY SAUCE, DIVIDED

2 TABLESPOONS BUTTER

3 CUPS COOKED RICE

2 EGGS, BEATEN

1/2 CUP FINELY CHOPPED GREEN ONIONS

1. Heat vegetable oil in a large nonstick skillet over medium-high heat. Add onion and cook until tender. Stir in garlic and cook for an additional minute.

2. Increase heat to high and sauté mixed vegetables, sesame oil, and half the soy sauce. Cook vegetables until they are heated through.

3. Move vegetables to one side of the skillet to make room for the rice. Melt butter and then add rice and remaining soy sauce. Toss and fry until the rice is crispy brown.

4. Push mixture to one side of the skillet and pour in beaten eggs. Using a spatula, scramble the eggs until they are cooked through.

5. Mix all the ingredients together and top with chopped green onions. Season with additional soy sauce, salt, and pepper to taste.

RIDE-OR-DIE SIDES

BALSAMIC BRUSSELS

This one will wow with essentially four ingredients and almost zero prep. The oven does the work for you, allowing the balsamic to caramelize, the Brussels to brown, and the magic to happen. Don't be afraid to cook the heck out of these! It's the crispiest brown bits that are the hardest to resist.

1/4 CUP OLIVE OIL

1/4 CUP BALSAMIC VINEGAR

2 TABLESPOONS BROWN SUGAR

1/2 TEASPOON SALT

1/2 TEASPOON PEPPER

1 POUND BRUSSELS SPROUTS, TRIMMED AND HALVED

1 Preheat oven to 400 degrees.

2 In a large bowl, whisk together olive oil, vinegar, brown sugar, salt, and pepper. Add Brussels sprouts and toss to coat.

3 Spread onto a large baking pan and cook for 30 minutes or until crispy brown.

CABBAGE CRACK
WITH GOAT CHEESE

SERVES 6

I wouldn't dare make you eat cabbage unless it was knock-your-socks-off good . . . and this is! Like its namesake, it's highly addictive. I've been known to make multiple trips to the fridge long after it's been put away for hits of this tangy, buttery goodness. I'm not kidding when I say I could eat this every day.

3 TABLESPOON BUTTER

1 CUP WHITE VINEGAR

2 TABLESPOONS SUGAR

1 HEAD RED CABBAGE (ABOUT 2 POUNDS), ROUGHLY CHOPPED INTO BITE-SIZE PIECES

1 CUP CRUMBLED GOAT CHEESE

1   Melt butter in a large pot over high heat. Stir in vinegar and sugar and bring to a boil.

2   Add cabbage and toss to coat. Cover pot, reduce heat to a simmer and cook for 30 minutes or until cabbage is tender. Stir occasionally so the cabbage doesn't burn or stick.

3   Season with salt and pepper to taste. Sprinkle goat cheese on top.

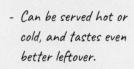

- Can be served hot or cold, and tastes even better leftover.

GOLDEN GARLIC POTATO WEDGES

SERVES 4-6

Golden, garlicky, and pillow-soft on the inside while crispy on the outside. Perfect to serve with steak, burgers, or wings.

- -

1/3 CUP OLIVE OIL

2 TEASPOONS GARLIC POWDER

1 TEASPOON PAPRIKA

1 TEASPOON SALT

1/2 TEASPOON PEPPER

2 POUNDS YUKON GOLD POTATOES, SLICED INTO WEDGES

2 TABLESPOONS CHOPPED PARSLEY, FOR GARNISH

1. Preheat oven to 400 degrees.

2. Combine oil, garlic powder, paprika, salt, and pepper in a large mixing bowl. Add potato wedges and mix well to coat.

3. Arrange wedges, flat-side down, on a baking sheet. Bake for 30 minutes or until golden brown and crispy, flipping potatoes at the halfway point.

4. Sprinkle with parsley. Season with additional salt and pepper to taste.

GREENS 'N BEANS

It doesn't get much easier than this! This is a filling, rustic, Italian classic that never gets old.

1/4 CUP OLIVE OIL

2 CLOVES OF GARLIC, MINCED

1-POUND BAG KALE, ROUGHLY CHOPPED, DIVIDED

1 CUP CHICKEN BROTH, DIVIDED

1/2 TEASPOON SALT

1/2 TEASPOON PEPPER

1 CUP FRESHLY GRATED PARMESAN OR PECORINO ROMANO CHEESE, PLUS MORE FOR SERVING

1 CAN (14.5 OUNCES) CANNELLINI BEANS, DRAINED AND RINSED

1   Heat olive oil and garlic in a large skillet over medium-high heat. Stir in half the kale and cover with 1/2 cup chicken broth, salt, and pepper. Allow to cook down, then repeat with the remaining kale and chicken broth.

2   Sprinkle grated cheese on top and simmer partially covered for 10 minutes.

3   Add beans and continue cooking until heated through.

4   Top with additional cheese before serving.

OLD-FASHIONED
MASHED POTATOES

SERVES 4-6

Somehow, mashed potatoes frequently end up taking the starring role when they were cast to simply be a supporting side. That's why mastering mashed potatoes is more important than you think. I like to use an electric mixer to make these extra smooth and velvety. But if you don't have a mixer, don't worry; you can use a good ol' fashioned potato masher. Grandma's mashed potatoes were the BEST, and she certainly didn't have any fancy gadgets or doohickeys.

2 POUNDS YUKON GOLD POTATOES, PEELED AND CUT INTO 2-INCH PIECES

2 TEASPOONS SALT, DIVIDED

3 TABLESPOONS BUTTER, ROOM TEMPERATURE

3/4 CUP MILK OR HALF-AND-HALF

1 TABLESPOON CHIVES, CHOPPED

1   In a large pot, add potatoes and cover with cold water and 1 teaspoon of salt. Cover and cook over high heat until potatoes are tender. Drain water and transfer potatoes to a mixing bowl.

2   Using an electric mixer, mix potatoes until light and fluffy. Fold in butter, milk, and remaining salt. Top with chives and season with additional salt and pepper to taste.

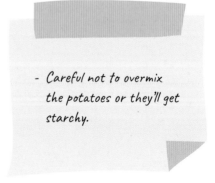

- Careful not to overmix the potatoes or they'll get starchy.

PARMESAN GARLIC STRING BEANS

Fresh green beans are a crispy complement to any meal. The Parmesan, garlic, and crunchy bread crumbs jazz up this simple side and can be thrown together in a snap.

. . . .

1/4 CUP OLIVE OIL

2 CLOVES OF GARLIC, MINCED

1 1/2 POUNDS FRESH GREEN BEANS

1 TABLESPOON BALSAMIC VINEGAR

1 TEASPOON SALT

1/2 TEASPOON PEPPER

1 MEDIUM ONION, CUT INTO THIN RINGS

1/4 CUP ITALIAN-STYLE PANKO BREAD CRUMBS

1/4 CUP FRESHLY GRATED PARMESAN CHEESE

1   Heat olive oil in a large frying pan over medium heat. Add garlic and cook for 1 minute.

2   Add green beans, vinegar, salt, and pepper and toss well. Cook for 15 minutes or until beans are tender and lightly browned.

3   Add onions and cook for an additional 5 minutes. Stir in bread crumbs and cheese. Season with additional salt and pepper to taste.

PICKLED SLAW

This is my summer side dish staple! I'm not a fan of mayo, so I absolutely love this sweet and sour alternative to your typical creamy coleslaw. This gets better with time and keeps for weeks in your refrigerator. This is a great side to bring along to a summer cookout or to just have on hand to add texture and tang to sandwiches, tacos, or just about any kind of barbecue food.

1/4 CUP VEGETABLE OIL

1/2 CUP WHITE VINEGAR

2 TABLESPOONS SUGAR

1/2 TEASPOON SALT

1/2 TEASPOON CELERY SEED

14 OUNCES SHREDDED CABBAGE OR COLESLAW MIX

1 SMALL ONION, FINELY CHOPPED

1. In a large mixing bowl, combine oil, vinegar, sugar, salt, and celery seed. Add cabbage and onion; toss well.

2. Cover and chill in the refrigerator until ready to serve. Mix well and drain out some of the excess liquid before serving.

CRISPY ROASTED BROCCOLI

Sometimes these don't even make it to the table because my family can't resist eating them fresh out of the oven. My kids devour these veggies like potato chips, and I feel like a supermom for giving them something healthy!

- -

1/4 CUP OLIVE OIL

1 TEASPOON GARLIC POWDER

1/2 TEASPOON SALT

1/4 TEASPOON PEPPER

1 POUND BROCCOLI, CUT INTO FLORETS

1   Preheat oven to 425 degrees.

2   In a large Ziplock bag, mix olive oil, garlic powder, salt, and pepper. Add broccoli and toss to coat.

3   Arrange broccoli on a large baking sheet and roast for 15–20 minutes or until crispy. Season with additional salt and pepper to taste.

Mix it up!

- Try adding 1/4 cup freshly grated Parmesan and 1/4 teaspoon of red pepper flakes before roasting.

QUICKEST CAULIFLOWER

When I'm really feeling strapped for time, I grab a bag of pre-cut cauliflower florets, season them up, and within minutes I've got a versatile and super healthy side.

. . . .

4 TABLESPOONS OLIVE OIL

1/2 TEASPOON GARLIC POWDER

1/2 TEASPOON PAPRIKA

1/2 TEASPOON SALT

1/4 TEASPOON PEPPER

1 POUND CAULIFLOWER, CUT INTO FLORETS

1   Preheat oven to 425 degrees.

2   In a large Ziplock bag, mix olive oil, garlic powder, paprika, salt, and pepper. Add cauliflower and toss until coated.

3   Arrange cauliflower on a large baking sheet and roast for 15–20 minutes or until crispy. Season with additional salt and pepper to taste.

ACKNOWLEDGMENTS

Oh $#!%, I wrote a book! But I couldn't have done it alone.

A huge thanks to everyone at Familius who took a chance on a first-time author and believed in me and my vision from day one.

Thank you to my incredibly talented photographer, Katie Ring, and my marvelously meticulous food stylist, Stacey Stolman.

A giant shout out to my ultimate cheerleaders, my family. My late grandparents, my parents, my bro, aunts, uncles, cousins, in-laws, and outlaws—this book is a tribute to each and every one of you. You are all over the pages of this book. Thank you for a lifetime of support, for always being my champions, and for the pep talks when I'd think, "Oh $#!%, what have I gotten myself into?"

A special shout out to Raylene Dill (a.k.a. Aunt Ray), my partner in culinary crime and my right-hand woman on this project. Girl, your consult and keys to the past are priceless.

A huge hug for my ride-or-die girlfriends (and real-life recipe testers) who helped me in more ways than they'll ever know. I'm so lucky to have you badass women in my corner.

Thanks to my fans and followers for all the support over the years and for giving me the guts to do this thing! It means so much.

And finally, my people, Josh, Grace, and Benjamin, who put up with piles of dishes, early morning and late night "cooks," and the many, many moods of a working mom on a book deadline. My sweet Bennie, you were always willing and ready to taste any food, any time. Nothing makes my heart smile like seeing you enjoy my cooking. Grace, my "consigliere," from helping me test to helping me type, you are my rock star. And Josh, you are my rock. Your love means the world to me. Thank you all for giving my life flavor.

ABOUT THE AUTHOR

MARIA SANSONE is an Emmy award-winning television host with an illustrious career in broadcasting. She is a social media personality, lifestyle expert, home cook, and mom of two.

Her genuine and authentic approach to broadcasting has won top honors and the hearts of many. A little sweet and a dash of snark, her no-nonsense style of cooking has made her recipes and digital content a social sensation.

From coast to coast, Maria has had an impressive television career spanning three decades. Thanks to winning a "slam dunk" contest, she got her start in front of the camera at just 11 years old and earned the title, "The Youngest Sportscaster in America".

Maria was the anchor of *Good Day LA* on FOX Los Angeles, a correspondent for *New York Live* on NBC New York and host of *The Hub Today* on NBC Boston. She's guest hosted *Live with Regis & Kelly, Anderson Cooper Live, EXTRA* and contributed to *Access Hollywood,* ABC, CBS, ESPN, TV Guide Network and has appeared on *The Tonight Show, Good Morning America, The CBS Early Show, Dateline NBC* and more.

Maria lives in a seaside town near Boston, Massachusetts, with her husband, Josh, and children, Grace and Benjamin.

ABOUT FAMILIUS

Visit Our Website: www.familius.com

Familius is a global trade publishing company that publishes books and other content to help families be happy. We believe that the family is the fundamental unit of society and that happy families are the foundation of a happy life. We recognize that every family looks different, and we passionately believe in helping all families find greater joy. To that end, we publish books for children and adults that invite families to live the Familius Ten Habits of Happy Family Life: *love together, play together, learn together, work together, talk together, heal together, read together, eat together, give together,* and *laugh together.* Founded in 2012, Familius is located in Sanger, California.

Connect

Facebook: www.facebook.com/familiustalk
Twitter: @familiustalk, @paterfamilius1
Pinterest: www.pinterest.com/familius
Instagram: @familiustalk

The most important work you ever do will be within the walls of your own home.